# THE
# EVERLASTING
## *Soul*

JESUS MEETS HIS SOUL

*Key boarded by*
# BILL MANNING

*inspired by*
### DIDYMOS JUDAS THOMAS

The Everlasting Soul by Bill Manning

This book is written to provide information and motivation to readers. Its purpose is not to render any type of psychological, legal, or professional advice of any kind. The content is the sole opinion and expression of the author, and not necessarily that of the publisher.

Copyright © 2018 by Bill Manning

All rights reserved. No part of this book may be reproduced, transmitted, or distributed in any form by any means, including, but not limited to, recording, photocopying, or taking screenshots of parts of the book, without prior written permission from the author or the publisher. Brief quotations for noncommercial purposes, such as book reviews, permitted by Fair Use of the U.S. Copyright Law, are allowed without written permissions, as long as such quotations do not cause damage to the book's commercial value. For permissions, write to the publisher, whose address is stated below.

ISBN 978-1-949746-00-6 (Paperback)
ISBN 978-1-949746-01-3 (Digital)

Printed in the United States of America.

Lettra Press books may be ordered through booksellers or by contacting:

Lettra Press
18229 E 52nd Ave.
Denver City, CO 80249
www.lettrapress.com
1 347-903-4909 | info@lettrapress.com

# Prologue

THIS BOOK IS about souls, the real you and me. They were around before humans became citizens of this earth. Likely our souls have been to earth more than once, living in other bodies. My soul lived here at least four times. One of those lives was that of Didymos Judas Thomas, the twin brother of Jesus of Nazareth. It is a voice from his past life, that of 'Didymos Judas Thomas' that reached out to me and asked that the real story of his brother Jesus be told. "Sit at the keyboard of the computer", I was asked, "and a memory you have never known before will become part of your mind.

This book is his story and that of his brother Jesus of Nazareth.

# Chapter One

JOSEPH WALKED ALONG a dusty, hot pathway, wiping sweat from his brow with his sleeve. It had been a long hot walk. A very impatient donkey travelled by his side. The animal, resentful, tired, and thirsty was pulling a cart loaded with the man's tools of his trade. When they passed others, it was not uncommon for them to call out a greeting. Such as; "Hello Joseph." If the face of the man was not immediately familiar, they certainly recognized the cart. It belonged to Joseph of Bethlehem; it seemed to tell all who saw it; "Need a new well, add a room, or even give good advice. Joseph is your man." By word of mouth, or just appearance his fame was legendary. He was known as a person who could just about fix anything, and that included entertaining at your wedding. Joseph of Bethlehem was an icon. Not only because of his all-around skill, but his congeniality and common sense made him good company. Joseph liked people, and they liked him. He was understanding and compassionate, his cart was distinctive, his personality compelling. You would know the vehicle as you would know Joseph.

The bearded man strode on, whistling through his front teeth. A happy man his four-legged friend accompanied the tuneless sounds of his master with the occasional bray

The day was hot for late autumn, and the roadway was dusty. The dryness had persisted for weeks, making people anxious and irritable. None more so than the donkey. Joseph understood his friend, and talked gently in its ear knowing the animal was hot and very thirsty, probably hungry too. Anyone who depended on a donkey in their work knew full well one should pay attention to these beasts of burden. It is well known donkeys will sit down in the middle of the road and refuse to move should their needs not be recognized. Joseph might well end up pulling the cart himself: so mused this carpenter handyman. If you were there to observe the smile that creased his good-natured face, as the notion flitted about his mind, you might smile also.

Joseph was thirsty himself. She (the donkey) had her last meal before they began the trip, now it was past midafternoon. It takes so little to raise the ire of any donkey at the best of times, and Geddy, (the donkey's name) being a living example of this rule, rather than the exception, was indeed hungry.

"We will be there soon old girl." He said this, while at the same time rubbing the beast's mane. As he did this he noticed dust created by the movement of his hand. Reinforcing his own desire for food and drink. He had a bottle of water in the cart, but when he thought of water fresh from a cool well, it pushed him to plod on.

"We are going to our next job, and we'll be there awhile, so you will be able to take it easy and get lots of rest while I work. You'll get a drink of good well water and sweet grass to eat. Then, my friend, you can sit in the shade of an olive tree, and watch me." Joseph could picture Geddy sitting on her haunches like a dog refusing to budge, as she had done before. The memory caused him once more to chuckle. A good friend and in a manner of speaking a business partner, a companion for many years. The two travelled together from one village to another, fixing, building, and digging wells. They were welcome guests in an area that covered a large part of Canaan. Joseph was also known far and wide for his entertaining stories, and good humour. The reputation of his expertise and good company passed from family to family; he was seldom without a job.

They were just entering Nazareth as he talked to Geddy. Here was their destination, after having departed from Bethlehem, just about seven miles back. Joseph had decided to stop to fix a doorway on the way, or they would have been there sooner. He paused for a minute to trigger his memory. Joseph screwed up his face as he searched his brain for the information regarding the location of the next job. "I am to look for a white house that has had many additions and is about to get another," he mused aloud. "White house," he chuckled, "all the houses are white, I could use a better clue than that.

Searching his memory again for the directions; "a man named Jacob wants me to build a rooftop room for a daughter. One he hopes to wed to someone not yet on the scene," Joseph snickered at his own humour as he talked on to the beast of burden. The donkey lifted its ears and let out a moaning sound every little while. Whether to complain or possibly just to be sociable, Joseph appreciated the fact Geddy was at least listening.

"Look Geddy," Joseph said, pointing to a house that seemed to fit the description, "see all the additions. This house might be it. Now, we need to find a man called Jacob". A snort from the donkey, combined with the wiggle of its ears, indicated no more or less interest other than its about time. As Joseph spoke, a short round man appeared at the front door of the house in question. The man looked at Joseph. Recognizing the description of the man and wagon he had, called out a greeting of surprise. "Hello and welcome!

You must be the carpenter I had asked Elias to send my way. I did not expect you for another week, never-the-less, I am glad to see you my friend." He was dressed in white to help ward off the hot rays of the sun, just as was the carpenter. Jacob ambled out to the road to greet the traveler.

"I would not have been here this soon, Jacob." Joseph grinned back. "I am early because a well I was to dig had been put off indefinitely. And speaking of wells, my donkey would like to get a drink. She is old, tired, and thirsty. I guess hungry as well." Jacob smiled, reached out, and patted the donkey, who looked back at him with a cynical glare. Jacob pulled back his hand and led the travelers around to the back of the house, where there was a well and a barn. "We keep our animals in here," he said, pointing to a well-crafted wooden structure. "Except the sheep of course. Give this deserving creature a drink. The well is there. Help yourself to water, and inside the barn is all the food your donkey will need. Why don't you unhitch the cart and tend to your beast while I call Ethel my wife, and my daughter Mary? Both will be delighted to see you. We get so few visitors. The ladies are out in the orchard pruning trees but will be glad of a break in their labours.

Jacob departed, and Joseph was left to tend to Geddy. When he had taken his donkey into the barn, and helped himself to some cool water, he found a bench in the shade and sat down, slipping his feet out of his hot sandals'. Talking to himself once again, and glancing critically at the well, he noticed it seemed to be as old as the house. "The well needs work, the house needs work, all that along with the room they wish built, I can see we will be here awhile."

After what seemed like a long wait, he heard voices approaching and soon was rewarded as two women, followed by Jacob came through the trees. "Joseph, meet my wife Ethel, and my daughter Mary." The elder of the two women came forward and greeted Joseph with a friendly smile. Joseph extended both hands to her in a warm greeting. To maintain proper decorum and not offend his host, Joseph paid not the slightest mind, to the young girl, who was obviously the daughter. It took all his inner strength, as Mary was indeed very charming. She, stood back shyly, with eyes cast down, as was proper, while at the same time adjusting her shawl a little closer to her face. At last Jacob said, "And this is this is my last unwed daughter, Mary. The girls face turned tomato red until Joseph's aplomb turned the embarrassing situation into a happy occasion by saying, Jacob, you are lucky to have had her company this long. Count your blessings." And with this, he stepped forward and took both of her hands in his and said, "Mary, it must be for you I am going to build a room on the roof." Jacob quickly interrupted and said, "Let us have some food, and then I will show you what it is we want. Yes, the room is for my daughter Mary. Ours is a large family and we have built additions to this house for generations, and now we will need to build up rather than out."

That was the day Joseph met my mother. He immediately fell in love with her and she with him. They often shared the memory of their first meeting with each other. True they did not know it was love in the beginning, but during the three months' father worked on the house, their love for each other was forged. In later years as our family grew, both mother and father would recount that moment with all of us children as we sat together. Joseph was her first and only love she would relate. Always with the same warm look on her face. I loved to see her expression as she recalled those pleasant memories. She was thirteen years old then and ready for marriage. That was the age most woman married. It was the custom in our land. Although father was many years her senior, it was his maturity and strength which drew her to him. On his part her delightful, happy, personality matching his own, attracted him. Mother was considerably more mature and serious than her young age would usually suggest. She was ready and capable to become a wife. I never believed differently, God had a hand in their meeting.

Weeks later Mary could climb new stairs that ran on the outside of the building. She did so every day. Stopping and marveling at the smoothness of the new wood, delighted by its scent. Mother sat with a dreamy smile on her face, as she related to the family how she trailed her fingers along the railing, day-dreaming. She just wanted to watch this man at his work. She admitted to us that she admired the confidence he displayed on the job, and the perfection of his work. She saw him as a person reliable in all situations. Here was a strong man whose character spoke for itself. The fact he was older than her never crossed Mary's mind. This, mother assured us more than once. It was easy for my brother and me to see her as having been mature at thirteen. She ruled the family with love and understanding, my brother being the outspoken person he was, learned the hard way. She told us of the many conversations, her and father had discussing their beliefs and hopes for the future.

Mother wanted a large family, one steeped in the Jewish faith. Father wanted that too. It was then he told her of his previous marriage, and his two children. 'Divorce will not be a problem Mary.' Joseph was quick to explain. Holding her face in his big hands he assured her the two of them together could deal with it. Our grandfather often said they were born for each other.

Joseph had an easy way of talking, and Mary loved to listen, he was a storyteller. To a young girl who had never left Nazareth, he appeared to be a man of the world, mature, confident, and reliable. Mother told us she was in love for the first and last time of her life.

As the days passed their fondness grew each day. Mother found herself visiting the roof to spend time with this amazing man. He was competent, strong in his opinions, but fair and compassionate. His actions told her he was also very thoughtful. She knew instinctively she was in love, and he returned that love. Mother risked her mother's sharp tongue when she neglected her work on the farm, but her instincts drove her to be with this man every moment she could.

As the weeks flew by there was no doubt in their minds they were destined to be together. Their conversation soon turned to talk of their marriage and Josephs current marriage. Which once more, our father again hastened to tell her; "This will not be a problem for you, your family or the entire community. Marriages can be ended quickly with the return of the dowry to the bride's parents along with my intentions in writing. Plus of course, the aid of a rabbi."

As Mother dreamed of the future, she sensed this was to be a marriage of destiny. She told him about dreams she had. He told her how his were similar. They knew their time together would be short because of the nature of his work, so they made the most of what time they had. It was going to be difficult for Mother to see him leave Nazareth to go off to work, but she knew this was what he did and told him she understood. They would sit on the top step and look at the night sky, Holding each other close. And so, it was on a clear cold starry night in Tishri 1 (January) that in the light of a full moon, up on the roof Mary conceived.

# Chapter Two

WHEN MARY DISCOVERED she was pregnant, she knew she must tell her parents. While she had already shared the knowledge of their intentions to marry, it was time to tell them of her pregnancy. The parents knew of Joseph's previous marriage. They had many discussions together on the increasing involvement they had witnessed between the young couple. Now they assured Mary and Joseph they would continue to support the with their customary understanding. Divorce at that time was not uncommon and easily accomplished. But some action must be taken soon. So, they immediately announced the betrothal of their daughter to Joseph of Bethlehem.

Father was away for six months, and by the time he arrived back in Nazareth, Mother was large with child. Her condition was no secret in this little town, unfortunately. But as expected in a tiny community such as Nazareth, talk of the pregnancy spread like wildfire, and the paternity was regarded with suspicion and much speculation. It was not unusual for a girl to be pregnant before marriage providing the father was a Jew. With Roman soldiers stationed nearby, on the lookout for female company, the community thought the worst. Most of the villagers put on their best smiles for the sake of mother's parents. But behind closed doors gossip raged rampantly. Father was far away, and Roman soldiers were seen on the roads regularly. They were hated and suspected of everything and anything. It was natural for many to think the worst. Therefore, much whispering took place in this small community, resulting in much finger pointing. Our mother was seen in the eyes of the village to have lain with a Roman soldier, and despite Joseph declaring the child as his, the townspeople labeled the baby a "mamzer" (bastard or outcast). Despite this, the young couple was still determined to marry.

The two children in father's former marriage were called James and Jude. With the dissolution of that marriage, they would come with him to live in Nazareth this being the custom, male children would remain with the father. So, Joseph told his wife they were divorced, issued a certificate, and returned the dowry to her parents. Now Mary and Joseph were free to wed in Nazareth. That was how it worked it was the custom, and it was their wish.

Thus, he left his home in Bethlehem taking with him his sons James and Jude and walked the seven miles to his new home in Nazareth. Here he began his new life, while they all awaited the baby.

Because of the mood of the people in Nazareth, the family felt things would work better if they travelled to Bethlehem for the birth. The circumcision ceremony to follow immediately after the birth. Mother knew this ritual would assure her child a place in the community of Israel. The bond of blood united all Jews, even those of the mamzer caste.

As the day grew nearer, they set off on foot to walk to Bethlehem. Mary rode part of the way on a donkey. Due to her swollen belly, there was a concern the trip could be hard on her. For this reason and to help deliver the child, Mary's mother, Ethyl, accompanied this little procession, leaving James and Jude at home with Jacob in Nazareth.

On a crisp October twenty third at midnight, a baby made its entrance to the world. My parents had decided to call their child Jesus if it should be a male, they never told me what they would name a girl. It was a proud Joseph that held the new arrival. Gazing at their beautiful baby both Mary and Joseph were extremely surprised when Ethyl, the new grandmother, suddenly exclaimed, and quite loudly, "Look! There is another about to come." It was at this point I made my grand entrance into this world.

Twins!

That stopped all conversation for a moment or two. Father looked at this new entry into the family and then at the one he was holding in his arms. We were identical. Mother told us later, we were born exact duplicates and remained so all our lives. The three adults needed to come up with a name and they did, I was named Thomas, or Tum. Throughout our lives, Jesus and I looked so much alike, we were often mistaken for each other, although it was only in appearance. I was calm and quiet; Jesus was determined to be heard right from the start.

Our parents held their two boys, ready to have the covenant with Israel marked into their flesh. The circumcision ceremony would be performed by a highly-respected elder. He left departed immediately with the blood and foreskin to quickly bury them. These were considered unclean as was the person who performed the operation. He was deemed unclean until he had completed this task and washed. After the twin birth and circumcision ceremony, we all traveled back to Nazareth. To live together as a larger family than had first been expected. Their first-born son was named David Jesus and I as the second born was called Didymos Judas Thomas, my one name-meaning twin in our Aramaic language and the other twin in Hebrew.

# CHAPTER THREE

WHEN THE GROUP arrived back in Nazareth, mother and father discovered traveling to Bethlehem for the birth of their sons had not altered how the people here viewed their new born. We were mamzer children of suspected paternity, and it stuck. Such men and women lived in a caste apart. Unable to marry within the established bloodlines of Israel. That would be more crucial to Jesus in later years than me. Because of this designation, the Rabbis would order us exempted from the religious life of our community. All throughout his young life this exclusion went a long way in shaping the thinking and attitude of my brother. Even though our family was a part of Nazareth life, the town still believed mother had lain with a Roman soldier. That was unforgivable in the eyes of all Jews. Jesus and I often talked about out exclusion. He became bitter toward the priests and rabbis, as for me I just did not care. While this exclusion did help to a little to steer the course of my brother's life, I believe it was God who had chosen him before he was born to follow the path he did.

From the time, he was old enough to understand, Jesus felt the hostility of the community. Being on the receiving end of the side-glance stares, the snippets of gossip, the giggling behind cupped hands and being shut out of mainstream society, pushed Jesus to seek God. I often wondered, had the community accepted Jesus and I as full members of the general population, would Jesus still have become the great man and leader he had. In retrospect, I would say yes, there could be no doubt my brother would still become the teacher and prophet he did.

Our father, Joseph, was not as demonstrative in his affection toward the boys, as he was to his daughters. He expected us to grow up quickly, and be men. If you are wondering why I say daughters, yes there were girls born into our family later.

My brother challenged authority early in life. He was quick to see the unfairness upheld by the gossip mongers in the community. Jesus would go out into the night and pray to God, asking for guidance and understanding. During the day, I would see him stop, and looking upward, just talking to God, like one would a friend. There was never a doubt in the family, but my brother was chosen for a special task. It was as though the hand of God was always on his shoulder.

While we both realized the population's attitude toward us was here to stay, I just shrugged it off. Jesus became rebellious toward the priests and elders in the community early in life.

And why not! We were not allowed to attend religious ceremonies, not even when our father died. We were twelve then. It hurt to see James, Jude, and mother go to the Synagogue without us. Just another blow. He often told me that someday he would right the many wrongs of those whose narrow minds divided people with manmade rules. Despite all of this, we were a close family. The foundation was our mother and her love. When Joseph, our father, the head and the leader of our family died, we lost our anchor and rock. It was left to mother to fill the role of both mother and father.

Even as I tell this story, I remember my father so well. His voice could be soft and encouraging or when angry almost a growl. His mind keen when planning buildings or fixing them, was loving and compassionate when we needed him. Mother was his love, we were the power that kept him going. Looking back, I can still see him, not tall, but stocky, well built, born with long arms and big hands. His legs slightly bowed, which caused him to walk with a rolling gate. His hair and beard were black, his eyebrows stood out so far from his face, they often-collected dust and shavings from the wood he worked with. Father was a hairy man. It covered his arms, legs, chest, and even down his back. We children would laugh and call him monkey man. He loved it and would chase us with a little hopping motion, allowing his arms to hang at his sides while his hands opened and closed. He was affectionate and playful, with all his children when we were little, but as we matured, so did he. He became more reserved and less emotional, perhaps living more within himself. I feel the attitude of the community played a large part in his outlook to outsiders. He had been known and loved by all, but the local community shut him out, as it did us.

During playtime, I would often stop and look to see Jesus standing off to the side, alone; thoughtful. It would cross my mind to wonder; What he was thinking? Did he feel left out of our games, or, even at that young age, did he see things in his future? If father had trouble showing affection, I noticed Jesus did too. Strange really; when I look back and see how he could love all the entire world, yet still feel alone within his family? But then God had not worked on him yet.

Jesus was compassionate and loving with mother, who when we were little, would hold both us boys on her knee, and tell us stories of our Jewish history. Mother was the root of family love. She loved everybody and everything. Jesus adored her; he wanted to hear as much about our ancestors as he could. My brother had such a strong need to learn as much as he could about our Jewish background. Especially, the link to King David. Later the unfairness he saw in our religious teachers disturbed him. Their presentations clashed with stories of Moses and King David and the building of the temple. Why did a boy find so much fault with our priests and rabbis? They never taught us. We were outcasts. We learned much of the local Rabbis teachings through James. He attended classes.

We learned how and why an earlier temple had been torn down and ravaged. Like all Jewish boys, we reveled in hearing tales of the great Kings. As mother taught us the story of Abraham and his two sons, we sat in total awe. The story of Moses and the Ten Commandments must be learned and burned into our memories. We would compare our history with today's situation with the hated Romans.

Mother was short, round, and beautiful. I adored her. I can still feel her touch and remember the scent of her body as Jesus, and I sat on her knee. While I loved cuddling, Jesus would squirm to get down unless he sat alone upon her knee. It seemed he wanted all her attention or none. She, had large brown eyes that always seemed to be smiling. Mother was love. Everyone loved her and delighted in her company. I include many of the townspeople as well as our family. You might think that to be an odd statement, considering the way some of the others shunned us, but few could shun mother.

She was the favorite of her father, Jacob, who was always bringing her little gifts. People today would call her a daddy's girl. Mother loved God with a passion. She would often raise her eyes to the sky when picking fruit from a tree, and with a smile, would mouth a thank you. Both parents taught us always to be grateful, not only to God but each other as well. "We have such a beautiful family my children, so we should thank God often."

Mother never believed God was a vengeful God, but forgiving and loving. She felt God knew humans made mistakes and would be happy to forgive us when we sincerely asked him. God was tolerant; she would say, "but don't overdo it." She passed on to us the history that it was important we know. From Abraham to King Solomon. She did this repeatedly, so we would never forget it. "Galilean Jews are indentured, but not defeated," mother would tell us. "We burn with pride in a living memory of ourselves as the people of Israel. We descended from the patriarch Jacob, grandson of Abraham. We have tilled this soil and called the land ours for more than a thousand years. Fighting war after war, enduring defeat, genocide, and exile at the hands of foreigners. Our identity as Jews is bound up in the land and the covenant that made this land ours. This covenant is our last defense against Rome: Our strongest."

Jesus would sit and listen to her every word. His mind was like a sponge soaking up every bit, to be stored there forever. It was necessary for us to learn our history and keep it in our minds. Jesus could hear it over and over even though he knew every word. Few could read and write. So, it must be memorized.

James was learning to read and write, but for the rest of the family, this Targum was our way to pass down our history. It is what made us Jews, and in our minds, what has made us different. These special moments with mother were to live with Jesus and strengthen his Jewish beliefs for years to come.

James was a big brother, to whom we all looked up. He was expected to become a teacher and priest. For this reason, he was sent out to learn to teach. That meant father excused him from helping in his work, or even on the farm.

James was taller than the rest of us and walked with long strides. We thought he did this to imitate the priests and rabbis. However, we whispered it behind his back as Jesus and I giggled. Also, James seemed to be constantly in a hurry, for what reason we never knew. He wore his hair long and compared to father's black hair; James was a soft brown. When father passed away, James took over as head of the house. He was an impatient person and often had trouble keeping his cantankerous moods in check, especially with Jesus, who was also impatient. They often clashed. It was assumed he would eventually move to Jerusalem to work in the Temple.

# Chapter Four

MY STEP-BROTHER JUDE, the second son of Joseph, was introverted: No! He was just shy with strangers, that is. Outside of home he had little to say. He did a lot of thinking. Because he was a good listener and had a marvelous memory. He was very aware of what was going on around him especially in our little world. You never knew what was happening in his head, because of that, some thought him to be a little slow. He was not. Careful, cautious, and very sensitive, and very loving. When he sat quietly without speaking, our mother would often say, "What have you been thinking about Jude?" He would look up at her, with a soft little smile on his face and shyly say, "Lots of things." He could neither read or write, yet he created poetry, which he recited and sang at family gatherings. James put much of his poetry into writing. Jude's eyes would fill with tears at the slightest provocation. He was an artist and emotional. A natural farmer, never to become a carpenter. Jude was born to live with the earth and its creatures. He would pick up a newborn lamb, and hold it up, and see God in the creature and say; "Look Thomas, and you will see God in his eyes." Everyone loved Jude, and he, in return, loved everyone, and everything. "This earth we live on belongs to God," he would say. "We are but tenants." Then go on to add: "Treat this land we live on with respect, and it will provide." I once saw him take up a handful of earth and kiss it. Then lifting his eyes to heaven, he would say, "Thank you, God." If one could not love Jude, no love lived in that heart.

Mother had four more children after Jesus and me. There was Ruth, who was born with a deformity on her upper lip. That caused her to become very shy with people. We all loved her and felt very protective on her behalf. She was fathers' favorite child. The love he held for her shone in his eyes every time he picked her up. When he would come back from a long trip, the first thing he did upon entering the house was to seek out Ruth.

Then there was Simon, who died at ten soon after mother returned from Jerusalem. Rachael and Beth were the second set of twins and died at six years of age. They were four when father died. These last two were the charge of Jude. This by his preference. He wanted to be a second mother to them and they loved him. Rachael and Beth would be with Jude whenever he was working on the fruit trees or with the new lambs. They had never been healthy and when they died, Jude wept and grieved for days.

Because the community rejected Jesus and me, James took on the task of teaching us. Jesus was very anxious to learn, but he was an abstruse student. Jesus wished to know more but questioned everything. My brother would not accept anything verbatim. He needed to take it apart and put it together again until he understood it. That made teaching him an unrewarding student. Add to that James was an impatient teacher. For instance: Jesus might say, "I cannot believe that came from God, it is not something God would say." James would become frustrated, and tell Jesus, abruptly, "you do not know what God would do and not do, what I am teaching you is acceptable in the eyes of the Rabbi's."

Jesus responded by saying that he did know God. "There is a difference between what God says and the words of the High Priest."

Like, mother, Jesus believed God was a loving God, not angry, as some of the teachings suggested.

James accepted everything the Rabbis' told him. Thus, the arguments never ended. Jesus would quietly remark to me he needed a new teacher. Sometimes, Jesus would say, "I do not say it is all wrong, but I challenge the interpretation." Jesus seemed driven to learn and would go out in the dark and under the stars and pray to God for a proper teacher.

James talked about the temple in Jerusalem, saying "This is where God lives." Jesus would respond with, "God lives everywhere." "Wait until you get their young man," James would come back, "There is a room called the holiest of the holies, which is God's room. Just see what you have to say when you are there." As it turned out that day was not far away. Our family was one of a few chosen to go to Jerusalem.

# Chapter Five

JERUSALEM, THE TEMPLE, and the Holy of Holies. Here is where we might find God's own room.

Oh, miracle of miracles, we were going! We had known a year ago, we were one of the families chosen to make the trip. The knowledge of which had been a continuous piece of conversation. Adding to our excitement, we will arrive in time for the Day of Atonement and the Festival of Sukkoth, or Tabernacles. In our village, only a few families can leave at one time. The selection of only a few families, is necessary, because, in the fall of the year, people are needed to harvest the crops. We work as a community and what we grow must feed all of us for a year. This rotation will only allow our family to make the trip to Jerusalem once in twenty years.

Jude would stay home and look after the livestock and the rest. It was his preference to remain at home. It was not a hardship for our brother. He was the dreamer, the composer, the one who lived in his mind. The thought of the travel, and the crowds, only frightened him. Ruth also preferred to stay at home. She was sensitive, because of her face, and of course, she loved Jude so dearly and wanted to be with him. She would never be comfortable with strangers. The other two girls and Simon were not well enough to travel. Mother would only leave them because of the knowledge Jude was there to look after the farm and all those staying behind. "Jude will remain home and taking care of the rest of my little flock." She said. As I said before, he was like a mother to the children.

To say we were excited is an understatement. Jesus and I were exuberant. We piled on all the clothes we could wear. This simply because could not carry additional bundles. We were loaded down with our offerings of fruit, grain, and wine. Thus, the alternative was wear them. We began as a large group, later the families eventually separated, each maintaining their pace, and plans. Our little group wanted to push ahead. We would camp at the side of the road rather than stop at an inn. The nights were cool, and the extra clothing turned out to be very welcome. It was a five-day walk to Jerusalem at best. We would cross the highlands of Galilee, which somehow seemed familiar due to father's tales about the wells he had dug and the rooms he had built. He talked incessantly about the countryside in detail when he came home from a trip. It just seemed we had been there ourselves.

Most families brought along some livestock to sell in Hammath, a centre much larger than our village. I was both awed and amazed to see the size of the town. James told me to hold my enthusiasm until I saw Jerusalem. We brought our offering goat along to sell it here. All the families did the same. Doing it this way, we would have some money to buy a goat at the Temple, plus a bit for expenses. That animal would later be our official sacrifice to God. It might seem odd to bring an animal and sell it, only to buy another one later at the temple. To bring our own all the way to the temple would anger the priests and making them hostile. Of course, we wanted to avoid that. Also selling our animal early in the trip freed us of the very real possibility that a wild beast might grab ours during the night. Mother thought it was a good trade. The priests make money selling us sacrificial animals, and we had one less problem with which to deal.

Hammath was on an ancient trade route and the people here used currency in their daily lives. Back in Nazareth, we used a barter system. It was very unlikely we would ever have actual money in our possession. We exchanged goods or services, meat, grain, or even clothing. The citizens of Nazareth would never think of looking for profit either. My fourteen-year old brother could not accept the concept of commercialism by those whose duty it was to preach God's word. He saw it as pure greed. Remember we lived in a small part of the world. Although, many years later Jesus still viewed currency with much suspicion. Jesus saw greed as the opposite of God, and currency was greed.

From Hammath it was downhill and into the wilderness of the hostile Jordan Valley. Here wild animals lived in abundance. We camped here for our first night. Knowing that every night after that was a risk of wild animals and the very real danger of robbers. It would be necessary for one person to remain awake to keep watch while the rest slept. The farther south we travelled it became imperative we keep guard all through the night and the remainder of the trip.

Near the end of the journey, we reached an area where the river widened, and formed little pools. Here we could wash up, and make ourselves a little fresher. We were grateful for this opportunity to rid ourselves of road dust. Our destination was the town of Bethany, where mother had two older aunts, Miriam and Martha. We wished to arrive there as clean as possible; it was only good manners.

When we finally arrived at their house, Jesus and I found ourselves standing outside this strange door with mixed feelings. We were both nervous and overwhelmed. Remember, we had grown up on a farm, in a small community. Everything here was so unusual. However, Miriam and Martha were so glad to see the family; they quickly dissolved our nervousness. Further washing away our timidity we were served a most delicious and welcoming meal.

Jesus could never have known then, and it was good he didn't, that in about fifteen years, he would once more be their guest under less joyful conditions.

Tabernacle celebration was a family solidarity occasion, and our gathering was a joyous one. Because, Miriam and Martha, knew a year in advance, we were coming, they went to great lengths to prepare a wonderful welcome. They cooked a spring lamb, which was a delicacy saved for very special visitors. It had been James travelling to the temple months ago, for training, who advised them of our visit. They must have spent the entire year in the planning, judging by our celebratory reception.

The home in Bethany seemed large compared to ours back home. Even when we thought of all the extensions to our farm, their rooms made it all seem larger. Or perhaps it was just finding ourselves in another town and someone else's house, that had made it seem enormous. When we looked at the busy street, often filled with people, all of them appeared to be in a hurry. Jesus and I soon began to miss home.

Looking outside, I pulled Jesus to the doorway, and whispered to him, "Where are their fields and livestock? Then turning my brother about I exclaimed; Did you see the carpets on the floor? They must be wealthy." Jesus frowned and said he could not understand why the Holy One, would bestow so much wealth on people who did not care for crops or animals. We were farmers, and had a different perspective.

The next morning, James set out to buy a goat for sacrifice. He walked to Jerusalem where there would be vendors close to the Temple. It was necessary to go to an area near the north gate, which was close by the Roman fortress.

James shuddered as he passed it. Like all of us, the spectre of Rome was a constant and frightening reality. Although he was more experienced than the rest of the family in dealing with merchants, he was not comfortable in their company. That was because it required bargaining and haggling which even for James was unfamiliar. These merchants were made to pay a percentage of their profit, to the high priest. That made buying an animal even more expensive. James tried to cover up his insecurity with a thin veil of haughtiness. All of that made little difference in the final price. Later back at the house, James, regaled us with side-splitting laughter, when he replayed his haggling prowess. Jesus and I just sat and giggled.

It was the hope of James that one day he would be accepted by the high priest to become part of the temple staff. Because it could happen that he would find himself in that role, James also attempted to show his sophistication and appear as though he belonged.

If James was somewhat insecure, he was also a proud man. A farm boy in a big city who was not willing to concede anything. It was important to him that he do the right thing at the same time not be taken for a bumpkin. Therefore, his plan was to look for an animal that would cost the least, but also please God. Never-the-less it was easy for vendors, to see him as being from a small farming community, and overcharge him. James did not wish to deprive God of a proper sacrifice, but he believed God would know we were not wealthy and understood his need to be thrifty.

Finally, having decided on a goat, he took it directly to the Temple, to be inspected by the priests, who would decide on the suitability of the offering. (The ever-insistent Jesus had argued, when you buy from one priest why would a second priest need to inspect and approve it if the seller was also a priest. Who was honest? Who was dishonest? What Jesus did not know, the seller was a merchant.) My suspicious brother. It was also customary to leave some currency for the merchant along with the price of the offering. In today's world, you would call it a tip. However, James was not inclined to do so, and after fastening a rope to the goat he turned on his heal and quickly fled through the north gate not looking back.

The family planned to present the remaining offerings of grain and wine personally. James headed to the south entrance, to meet the rest of the family, as well as some of the town's people. He would have liked to hand over the animal at the point of sacrifice, so the offering would be known to come from our family. But the priests were far too busy to allow this to happen. "Surely God would know it was from us," Jesus snapped, "All this providing our God agrees with the concept of sacrifice."

It was time and the walk seemed forever as we hurried to meet James, at the south end of the Temple, our excitement had mounted to a fever pitch. None of us would ever forget the next two days. Jesus and I were practically jumping. Except for James, the family had never been this far away from home. Here we were in Jerusalem, which to us is the centre of the world. The site of the building alone transfixed us. It gleamed white in the sun; the stonework seemed to sparkle, as the walls reached up almost to the heavens. The sun glinted off the gilt of the enormous Sanctuary, which was said to be the largest building in the world

Mother told us that in the room called the Holy of the Holies, no human was ever allowed to enter, except the High Priest, and that was only once a year on the Day of Atonement. And this was the Day of Atonement. We felt so blessed to be here where God lives.

All of us had been thinking of nothing else since leaving home, and could not wait to see this exceptional part of the temple. I wonder that if Jesus, had had the opportunity, would he have just entered this Holy of Holies, on his own, not as a sacrilege, but because of his closeness to Abba, the Father. I knew then, my brother, was a chosen person. Here was not something anyone else was likely to understand. Jesus felt so comfortable with God; his closeness was like family. If God were to make an appearance, where others would fall to the ground, to avoid looking at the face of God; Jesus would drink in His presence and send his love with his eyes. My brother was indeed very different. I had felt this from very early in our lives. I can only add; I see this as a positive difference.

Of course, Jesus knew it would have been impossible to enter this most sacred room. I only made the comment to explain the comfort my brother felt where God was concerned.

(Fifteen years later, Jesus would tell you, God would wish you to feel comfortable in the presence of his love. Rather than prostate yourself.) Thomas

The Holy of Holies was well guarded. Anyone trying to enter would be executed. Roman soldiers, or anyone for that matter not Jewish, would not be allowed inside the temple. There were Jewish guards, dressed very much like Roman soldiers standing guard. This choice of uniform was sanctioned by the high priest and preferred, both by the son of Herod, and Pilate. The Jewish population despised it.

Sacrificial offerings had become the temples main purpose. Logical thinking would expect the real purpose would be to bring people together to worship God. Offerings that were a sacrifice by the worshippers is part of our history. That is the absolute gift one could give to God. However, even at his young age, Jesus had his doubts about the sincerity of the High Priest. I am sure I told you this before, but I would expect he was the only fourteen-year old to think this way. I believe even then his thinking was beyond his time. He opposed taking food that could feed hungry people, burning it on fire where it would be no good to anybody, and call it a sacrifice to God. How could God benefit from this? Looking back on this, I would guess that fourteen years later he might be expected to have such an opinion. Did I say, he was before his time? There can be little or no doubt; he was a very exceptional human being.

Adding to my brother's opposition was the common knowledge that much of the sacrificial flesh would later be sold, for a profit to vendors, who then sold it for profit. What is worse; non-Jews, even Romans could buy it. Opinionated! There can be little doubt. But when I stopped to consider his point of view it made sense to me. He believed a person should talk to God in prayer, and often. Do it with feeling and love, openness, and understanding, like you would a close friend. This type of sincere devotion would connect you to oneness with the Almighty. I knew what my brother was thinking, I guess I always did. Jesus never felt it was necessary to approach God through another person. Face the Almighty on your own. When you wanted forgiveness don't go to anyone but God.

If the meat from the sacrifice, were made available to the poor and homeless, it would make some sense. But when non-Jews could buy it, and the proceeds go to the already wealthy, my brother strenuously objected. If some thought Jesus appeared contrary to general beliefs at that age, he was to undergo many more changes in his philosophy regarding his interpretation of the traditional teachings. All of which was only to widen the chasm between him and the Jewish leaders. There was never any doubt in my mind Jesus considered himself to be a good Jew.

# Chapter Six

TO MAKE OUR way to the temple, we climbed the hill that led towards the Holy Building itself. Mount Mariah. As we looked up and ahead to the edifice itself, I could not help but recall what Mother had told us about this structure. Before us was the second Temple built on this very spot. King Solomon, the son of our beloved King David, built the first temple. It had been a dream of his father. The magnificent edifice involved massive amounts of building materials plus a vast amount of funding to complete the construction. The temple of temples, built for the glorification of God. I thrilled to know this is the very site where Abraham, the father of our faith, offered his son Isaac up as a sacrifice to God.

King Solomon's temple unfortunately, was not to last. King Nebuchadnezzar of Babylon looted it and took all the valuables back to Babylon. Later he ordered it destroyed. He had further ordered his soldiers to take away all written evidence the building had ever existed. They failed in this. The detritus and ruin had lain there for years as proof of his crime against the Jewish people. Our mother told us this story many times, so we would never forget it. No Jew should. She always related it as she had learned it, word for word. Jesus listened with rapt attention, asking question after question.

My brother was to repeat this piece of Jewish history often when talking to his followers about the needless waste of war. Just as mother had taught us, he later was to weave it into his sermons. The destruction of this temple became a rallying force for all our people. This act of treachery would to be remembered by Jews forever.

The second temple we were about to enter, had been built using exiles who had escaped slavery or been released by the Babylonians. The original foundation had been laid about five hundred years before our time. When King Herod took the throne, he had his builders use that very detritus that lay around the foundation in the building.

King Herod, whished to gain favour with our people. So, he offered to rebuild and restore this temple into something even bigger than the last. In this he succeeded. The king's proposal met with great rejoicing and support. Herod was true to his word, the exterior and interior was lavish in the appointments. He pushed the construction along and completed the main section in about ten years. There was still much to be done when we arrived. As unfinished as it was, its glory took our breaths away.

Herod could not be anything but himself; he wanted to play to every audience. For the Jews, he built the temple, for Mark Anthony he placed a great eagle, the emblem of the Romans, and for Tiberius, he enlarged Jerusalem by extending the wall around the city. While the Jews loved the temple, the eagle was an affront, and it only increased their hatred of King Herod.

The King died when we were about four years old, and his grandson Herod Antipas, succeeded him. Antipas was a Tetrarch meaning one quarter. There was a power struggle and his quarter share of Herod's kingdom, was Galilee, east bank, and Perea.

As the power was in transition, three men, all of them shepherds, each, and on his own, gathered together armies of Jews, to revolt against the Romans. One of them a man named Simon, from the town of Perea, fought courageously, and came close to defeating the Roman army, but in the end, was no match for the well- trained soldiers of Pilate. Finally, he fell in battle, dying in a stony ravine, where no vegetation existed, or water entered. The Roman soldiers left his body unburied in this stone filled dusty gulley as a warning to all who would defy Rome's might. Three days after his death, his followers, claimed, to have seen his spirit rise from his body. They proclaimed him as the Messiah, saying his soul had risen from his dead body and was now with God. They prophesied his Spirit would lead them to freedom, from the hated, Roman invaders. Our young brother, Simon, was named after him.

When we grew close to this wonder of wonders, we strained our eyes to see ahead, despite the Temple itself being far above us, and still a distance away. The closer we got, the greater were the crowds. They gathered around us, pushing and shoving. Coming from such a little community we were unaccustomed to people, in such masses. The many different cultures amazed both Jesus and myself. You might wonder how coming from little Nazareth where there were only Jews, could we distinguish strangers. It was the colour and style of there clothing and the many foreign languages. The throngs of visitors from many different lands wore costumes we had never seen before. Who were they, and from where did they come? We spoke in whispers, hiding our mouths behind our hands. We did this even though no one could hear us. There had been nothing in our daily lives, no experience to compare with this wonder, or even prepare us. Filled with a blend of awe, excitement, and yes, even embarrassment we felt like little people in a land of giants.

The blend of smoke and burnt meat, began to blow down to us, filling our nostrils, making our eyes water this far down the mountain. Even though we were still more than a mile away. As uncomfortable as it was, all of this only fuelled the excitement that had been building for days. When we giggled at the way, some of the women dressed. Our mother spoke sharply to us, telling both Jesus and I we must show respect.

It was important to be clean, before heading up to the gates and into the presence of the Holy One. Before going into the temple, we needed to bathe. Pools at the foot of the Temple Mount allowed us to cleanse properly. Total immersion was required. At this point, we had already been climbing from Siloam, passing masses of vendors selling almost anything one would wish for themselves, or as a last-minute offering.

There were separate baths for men and woman, and strangely enough, for Gentiles. Male youths were herded off with their mothers. It was breath taking to see the system of canals and cisterns that brought the water to the baths; the engineering was ingenious. My father would have been very interested in the mechanics of this construction. How could anyone living in a little community such as Nazareth even grasp the enormity of this incredible edifice?

Finally, it was time for us to enter the Temple itself. I found myself clenching my jaws, and holding my arms and hands so stiffly they ached. It was the realization of our dream to be here in the house of God. Up until now, this was something we had only heard about. Not in wildest fantasy even dreamed could we have imagined what stood before us. Now our greatest hopes were about to be realized. Can you possibly imagine our excitement and our pride at being Jews? We trembled, our legs felt weak as we continued to speak in whispers, moving forward one step at a time. Our emotion left us both frightened and unbelieving. Were we worthy I asked myself? We were about to be in the presence of God. I was dizzy, with exhilaration; I know my twin brother was too.

Fighting to control our emotions, we mounted the very wide stairs and ascended carefully. Because of the multitudes of visitors climbing alongside us, pushing and shoving each other, a fall here would be hazardous. The stairs so steep. The height was dizzying.

So many people from so many countries, Gentiles as well as Jews, all were heading toward the gates above, clamouring to reach the top.

The clothing of many of the women was unlike anything we had ever seen before. Wearing jewellery that no woman in Nazareth would dream of owning. All we could do is gape and wonder. Romans from afar, all animated laughing talking even yelling loudly. The noise seemed offensive, or at least to us, and I am sure others who came from little country villages such as Nazareth.

Some Jewish hucksters, called out to Gentiles, claiming they could take them into the Temple. For a small fee, of course. It was a lie, non- Jews entering the Temple would be put to death. But surprisingly many accepted the offer, only to be turned back before they were allowed through the gate. That was just another example of the greed found in this holy place. A lust for money that had infiltrated this the home of the one and only God. Jesus did not fail to note this. On the one hand was the divinity of this holy sanctuary, and on the other, was the overwhelming commercialism. I admit, the significance of all this went by unnoticed by myself.

Standing shoulder to shoulder, I felt the shudder that ran through my brother; it was noticeable to me, perhaps not to mother. He and l almost in the house of God were trying not to stumble and fall. As people shouted, pushed and laughed, my brother said why do they mock Him? I had other things to think about and missed his point. Now after all these years I have a better understanding of his objections. I am sure much of this was instrumental in shaping his convictions.

In years to come, Jesus matured and some of his current views would change, or at least moderate, but his loathing of the worship of wealth instead of God only stiffened. As you will learn later. While Jesus saw the temple as strictly for the Jews, many years later he would state with conviction, God is for all people. It would take a lot of experiences to make this happen. In a discussion we had later, we then believed this had been part of the plan God had for Jesus. Now I know it was.

Gentiles, even though they bathed, were not allowed into the Great Court. Why they bathed at all, I never understood. Perhaps it was just to experience the baths. Understandably the system of the baths was unique. A lot of the things people were doing amazed me.

I should explain the gate was in fact a tunnel, built on a slope still moving upward. There were no windows for lighting so for us people to see there were blazing torches which burning continuously to give light. The smoke from the burning oil caused us to cough. The climb was the equivalent of four stories. I had never seen a building more than two so will admit the height itself was intimidating and scary. I was afraid of heights and never lost that fear.

Coming out of the dark into the sun as we left the stairway was a blow to the optic nerves, and we had to cover our eyes for a moment. Then as they gradually became adjusted to the brilliance we noticed how the dazzling display of sun made the gold and silver sparkle. It left us breathless.

We were assigned to stay with our mother and go into the court for women. The three of us looking around found ourselves near the Sanctuary of white marble, the Holy of

Holies. Jesus and I had talked endlessly about this moment since we had left home, I guess long before that. Now we were here in the place of which we had only dreamed. The excitement and rapid breathing and the smoke caused our throats dry and raspy.

Here was the ultimate moment of our lives and we were living it! Bewildered, jubilant, in awe. I do not know if I can describe fully how I felt. Even Jesus, who had argued earlier that the closeness of God could be experienced equally anywhere, could not deny this moment. I tingled from my inner core to the outer most area of my skin. I could feel each hair on my arms. It was almost painful. My skin felt both hot and cold at the same time, as it reacted to this unbelievable experience. I stood transfixed, afraid to breathe or even move. Was this fear, love, or panic? I was here in the presence of God. My eyes wanted to close but were afraid to miss something. From my toes to the hair on my head, the sensation was that of living in another life, in another body. This was God's home; his essence was all about us. I dropped to my knees along with my brother, and we held each other's hand. We would never be the same again. We wept from sheer joy, and the tears ran from our eyes to our mouths, the salt burning on cracked lips.

Looking around and attempting to take it all in I saw the inner court was a rough structure made of uncut stones. The walls were probably twenty or more feet high; it was within this I saw an enormous alter fire. This inferno was nothing more than a huge pit of blazing logs surrounded by young priests throwing wine, corn, and animals into this seemingly bottomless pit. All around were ramps where the priests worked. Smoke, ashes, embers and blood were spread around everywhere. The priests themselves dressed in what might, at one time, have been ornate robes now covered in blood and gore, even feces. The tops of their garments were peeled down to their waists, leaving their upper bodies naked. I could see their sweaty backs glistening in the light of the crackling orange flames. In the background, just out of sight, the sacrificial animals bellowed in fear, knowing death was in the air. Soon it would be their turn. The cacophony became a symphony of sounds complemented by the popping and splashing of fat. The singeing stench of burning animal hair, mixed with the smell and sound of the sizzling wine as it was poured into the flames. Smoke hung in the air, mixed with the smell of animals. Here our offering of wine and wheat was cast into this inferno and instantly disappeared. Our only acknowledgement of our gift was the burning of our eyes. If we thought it hot down below, up here it was infernal. Our lungs rebelled when we inhaled, but nothing could dispel the total incomprehension of the moment.

Jesus and I stared at all of this for a few moments, and then we moved away from this frenzy driven by the heat and foul air. Almost racing we soon found ourselves back at the Sanctuary. We had left mother to find a place where peace and quiet, prevailed. We still held hands, and stood in awe, as we realized we were indeed here. Now finally away from the sacrificial fire, with its horror, and into an area of peace. Well, a bit more peaceful. There were crowds around us. Despite this, we felt the tranquility of Gods love.

We who were labelled mamzer, we who had not been allowed to attend our father's funeral, were here in God's presence. During all of this, away from the killing and confusion, The feel of God's love, seemed renewed, and I was clutching it to me like a blanket. Delighting in the comfort, I know Jesus did too. I had not known or understood until then, what one with God,' truly meant, but my heart now felt it. For I sensed the rapture to be part of God himself. In that very moment, I felt the nearness of the Holy Spirit. But 'complete' understanding of that concept, would still be a long way off. Because my head was a jumble of thoughts, my body numbed by the experience, I asked myself what was it I felt outside of numbness? Was it just being a part of all this? Did I feel insignificant? I knew all of this was not merely a temporary exhilaration. I knew this was forever, I had grown, I had changed. With these thoughts buzzing about my brain I wandered alone around this huge building. This place was not a synagogue nor was it the temple I had imagined it would be. I needed to discuss this with my brother.

What was Jesus thinking? I turned to ask him and realized he was gone. I guess he might have been as confused as I was. Suddenly, I felt alone. Where was my mother? Where in this enormous building would I look? With so many people I didn't know where to start. Where was Jesus? I don't remember ever being so confused and frightened. It was imperative I found my mother and brother. I began to push myself through the crowds. Looking for both.

Later, years later, I learned he had wandered farther away and mixed with the crowd. His mind too was a mixture of thoughts. He needed to think, so he sought a place where he could be quiet and pray, try to understand, but mostly pray. There was too much happening inside the building, so he just went outside. That was no easy feat. He did not think about the rest of us. There was so much happening inside his head; he just knew he must find a quiet place. He pushed his way out through the big doors, fled down the steps. Now in almost shear panic! Away from all the merchants, no reason, just fear. We will never know what it was he feared. He just ran. Finally, he wandered without direction, seeking only to be alone. Escape from all the turmoil. Off the hill, not knowing or caring where he was, he finally sat down under a fig tree to talk to God. He told him about this place of worship, where God and greed worked side by side. This temple where he found true feelings of love, understanding, and compassion alongside avarice and thirst for power.

As he sat alone, he called out, "I am sickened by the presence of Roman soldiers, and tourists, even here on the outside. These are merchants whose only business is to sell and prosper. Their presence seems fundamentally wrong to me Father. Maybe I just do not understand." All this Jesus said to God aloud while people walked by, not even giving him a single glance. With hands, together in front of his face, he asked for understanding and guidance. "I need to learn so much, and I will not find it back home where there is nobody to teach me. I pray to you my father, for guidance, and promise I will do whatever it takes to become useful to you and all people."

It was many years later when Jesus and I were both men, he explained to me the mixture of emotions, rapture, revulsion, shock, and despair, brought on by this experience. It was this night that Jesus left, disappeared from our lives and none of us would see him again for almost fifteen years.

Jesus got up from that fig tree and began walking. He walked until he was weary. Completely drained from emotion, he realized he had not had food since morning. Thinking about his stomach, he also knew he was, alone and lost. Now not knowing what to do he just closed his eyes, tried to think, then finally off the road, pulled his robe around himself and slept.

At about the same time I found mother, then James appeared. We all decided our part in the sacrifice was over and it was time we went back to Miriam and Martha's house. Tired and hungry it was time to go. Mother turned to me and said, "Thomas, where is Jesus?" I replied. "I have been looking for him and cannot find him. He had been with me constantly and now is nowhere to be found. Perhaps he's exploring every corner and then some. You know his penchant for discovery." I added the last half-jokingly. But knowing his tendencies, we were more annoyed than worried. So, we searched everywhere, but my brother had totally disappeared. I was accustomed to chase him down, be the one to look for him. In the past, and I always found him. This time was different. Fear was beginning to grow in all of us. Mother was the first to be very concerned. Knowing Jesus tendency to do the unexpected she somehow knew this time it was different. Was it a mother's love and protectiveness, or did she have an inner fear that this very unusual son had done something he had never done before. That left her with a hollow feeling?

James came back from the all-male section, where he had gone to look. He informed us that he was not over there. Jesus had just disappeared. Gone. We searched everywhere, going over the places we had just looked. We asked the guards for help. James went to see some priests and elders. Jesus had vanished. Mother was now frantic as was James. A deep gnawing feeling in the pit of my stomach had told me this might happen. Perhaps it was something twins know, others don't. Or did I believe this was an answer to Jesus prayers asking God for help? It had been a conviction of mine from a long time back God had chosen Jesus for a special mission. I was afraid to mention my thoughts to anyone for fear of sounding foolish. Now I could no longer hold them back.

"Mother I think Jesus has left to find answers. I think I understand it now, or perhaps I always knew. My brother is not like the rest of us. He has been chosen by God and must follow the path his Master has planned for him."

"What do you mean left, Thomas?"

"I think he has gone off on his own to find the answers he has been unable to get anywhere else." I meekly offered this unsatisfactory explanation.

Mother would not accept this. Which is natural I guess, so after repeated searches produced no Jesus, we went back to the aunt's house in Bethany. They had not seen him either. Finally, after days of waiting, not knowing what more we could do, we reluctantly left for home. Back to Nazareth. What else could we do?

It was sometime on the trip home; mother suddenly became very calm and knowing. A total changed swept over her. God had come to mother in her sleep and told her all would be well. Her son was following his destiny. Even though she would not see him for years he would return. There was a different look in her eyes. She had found peace. She told us of her dream the next morning. That confirmed what I knew had happened. More than fourteen years would pass before we were reunited.

When we returned to Nazareth, life resumed its regular course. As for me, I would carry on my father's work as a carpenter for only a short while. An extraordinary thing took place, well for me it was extraordinary. I ordinarily do not jump into things entirely new. For a reason I can't explain, my life took a strange turn. First, I decided I wanted to learn to read and write. Most of the population never thought of doing this. However, a teacher became available along with an opportunity to learn the trade of ship building. That took me to the sea shore where I lived for many years. I never married, but travelled home whenever I could, to watch over our mother, and spend time with Ruth and Jude.

I missed my brother more than I can explain, but strangely often felt his presence. Perhaps he was thinking of me in those moments. When we were very young we would hold hand's promising to be together always. As it turned out, that was not to be. Our lives would take an unexpected turn. The twin brothers who looked so much alike, but were so unalike in aspirations, were to travel in many different directions. Jesus at the age of fourteen was to set off on a quest he could never expect would turn out as it did. That unshakeable faith he had in God, was with him to guide and protect him. Of that there was no doubt. God was about to take a hand and shape his life. The answer to his plea to God for guidance had arrived.

The events in the life of Jesus which I will relate from now until his return, I learned when Jesus arrived back in Nazareth.

# Chapter Seven

SLOWLY AND PAINFULLY Jesus opened his eyes. He had been lying just off the trail and he was clutching his robe tightly around himself, the air was damp chilly this time of morning. Something else was bringing him quickly back to his senses. That something he suddenly realized was pain. Added to this his teeth were chattering uncontrollably in the cold morning air. He struggled to grasp his situation. He was both hot and cold at the same time. Fear clutched him as he realized something was wrong with his left leg. The pain was intense. Confused and alarmed he struggled to sit up, attempting to have a closer look. He pulled up his robe and looked down at his leg. The calf was to twice its normal size. It was discoloured and throbbed all the way up to his thigh. Then as he moved to get his back off the cold hard ground and fully sit up in order to reach his leg, a hand gently held back the move. Now for the first time he became aware of a pair of brown eyes, looking at him with concern. Those eyes belonged to a face which gradually focused into a body. Looking closer, Jesus saw two strangers kneeling beside him, one holding his hand and another helping him to sit up.

A voice spoke to him in his language. That voice seemed to be explaining something. What was it they were saying?"

A viper has bitten you. You need treatment young master." The voice was soft and compassionate, reassuring. Despite the calmness of the words, Jesus was startled, alarmed, and pulling himself back he tried to speak. However, the one holding his hand spoke first.

"Do not fear; I promise you are in good hands and above all safe." Strangely reassured, Jesus relaxed, as he peered at coloured robes, maybe orange, or so they seemed in the morning sun. He was both bewildered and confused. Jesus thought his eyes must be playing tricks on him. He could do nothing but accept the ministrations offered. Which he gratefully did.

Later he was to learn they were Buddhist monks. Together, these men bent to help him up, and gently urge him to a shelter. He had no recollection of that being there the night before. Assisting him into the tent, they suggested he lay down on a carpet, which covered the floor. Gratefully the boy sank to the ground, dizzy, in pain, confused, and feverish. Jesus had some difficulty making sense of any of this. Was the bite they had mentioned the cause of this anguish? Nothing mattered. He just fell back and surrendered to their offer of help and drifted into a welcome sleep.

When he eventually awoke, the young Jew had no idea how much time had passed. Through half opened eyes, he watched, as these two kind strangers worked on his leg. Seeing him once again conscious, one of them offered him water, which he eagerly and gratefully gulped down. His mouth was parched, his tongue seemed swollen, even his vision was distorted. The two saviours promised to give him food after the treatment. He knew he needed that too and was grateful. Where was he, where were his mother and the rest of the family? Jesus struggled to recall how he got here. He was unable to focus on anything. He pushed his memory until bit-by-bit little pieces of the puzzle came back to him. Visions floated in and out of his mind. He recalled the temple and his frustration with the noise, the chatter, the smell, and his feelings about the commercialism. Then in frustration and futility, he had fled. Was it all real? Did he do that? Then just as he was beginning to make some sense of it all, the scene began to fade away, and he slept once more, only to awake and sleep again. While he slept the travelers took advantage of his unconscious state to wrap leaves and plants around his leg.

Much later he awoke again, momentarily confused, then suddenly recalling the two strange men who had helped him. He struggled to regain control of his thoughts; he allowed his mind once more to recall yesterday. Or was it a few days ago? He recalled his flight from the temple to the streets, followed by aimless wandering alone not knowing where he was going. Then he remembered being famished. In desperation, he tried begging for food and received a slap for his effort. Humiliated and frightened he found himself out in the countryside and stopping here. He asked himself; had he really done this? Left his family and wandered to this place. But where is this place? He tried to make some sense of his present predicament. Should he attempt to explain what he was doing here? He was not sure could. It all seemed so unreal. He recalled once more the smell of blood, the screaming animals, the shouting people, the memory became a horror in his mind. It seemed so surreal. He tried to block it with good thoughts of God and that other side of the temple. The side where he and his brother prayed and felt the presence of God. The thinking was too difficult, best to forget it and just lay back. The effort of remembering was so tiring. He needed rest to recuperate from whatever was wrong with him. The strangers spooned some warm soup into him, then laid him back to sleep more.

He went to asleep thinking of his family, the love, warmth and what they must be thinking about right now. With that full realization brought him wide awake. What did they do when they could not find him? They must have been worried sick. They would have hunted for him for hours, only to find him gone. Jesus began to feel very guilty. Have I done the right thing? They would be anxious, to say the least. With a heavy feeling in his chest he lay there with his eyes closed. Afraid to open them and face the world. Everything seemed too much for this fourteen-year old fevered boy, who had never been away from home. Opening his eyes, he looked at these kind men who had been helping him, they deserved some explanation. With that and for the first time, he spoke to them to thank them for their mercy. Struggling to speak he tried to blurt out some form of explanation. He told them of his family, the trip to the temple, and how it had affected him. He told how he went there to be close to God, and what he found instead. The smells, the noise, the hypocrisy, and the commercial side of a place that is supposed to be holy. Finally, he said it had all become too much, and he ran away.

Jesus was surprised at himself, exposing so much of his inner thoughts. "I ran away because I wanted to find the truth and did not believe I would discover it back home." The gentle men in their orange robes attempted to calm their young charge. They were on their way to their home to a far-off land, they told him. They would be happy to stay with him until he could travel he was assure. Jesus could decide if he wished to return home or continue his quest. Until he was strong enough to decide, just rest and get well. Gratefully, exhausted and confused Jesus fell back and slept some more.

The monks watched him as he moved restlessly in his sleep. When he awoke on the third day, Jesus was hungry. He was glad to accept the rice soup which had been flavoured with leaves from a fragrant plant. It tasted so good and reminded Jesus how long it was since he last ate. At the same time, the monks changed the dressing on his wound again.

They applied a dark sticky substance to his leg and covered it with leaves. The cooking fire radiated warmth and was comforting. Amenities that made him feel much better. The resilience of youth quickly helped him return closer to his naturally curious self.

Jesus felt strangely comfortable in the presence of these kind men who called themselves monks. Yes, they evoked much curiosity in the young man from Nazareth. He wanted to know more about who they were and what they did. They were happy to explain again; they were Buddhist monks returning from Jerusalem. For the moment the answer sufficed their guest. Thus, the group of three continued to remain camped there on the edge of the city. Which gave the leg of Jesus a chance to heal and as it did, give his inquisitive mind the opportunity to kick into full speed, by asking many questions.

Early each morning the men would leave Jesus at dawn, then take their begging bowls and walk into Jerusalem where they asked for food. Explaining later, per their vows, they can only beg for food from dawn till noon. Then fast the rest of the day when the cycle begins again. Upon returning, they would share the food they had received with Jesus.

Seeing Jesus was still confused, the monks explained the reason for these actions. They told him of their great founder The Buddha, the awakened one, who had been born a prince with the given name of Siddhartha. The Buddha, they continued, said that for followers to feel part of their religion, they may do this by sharing. It is the duty of the monks to allow others to share their own abundance, by giving to the holy orders. All humanity should learn and love to share what they have, including compassion for the unfortunate. Jesus listened carefully to all of this, and despite his innate caution, it made a lot of sense to him. He believed these were men of God, and yet they were not Jews. It suddenly became evident to him that one need not be a Jew to be Godly. Were all Buddhists like these two? Jesus took his first step toward an open mind.

As he began to feel much better, the monks discussed the actions Jesus had taken that brought him here. They told him they had felt he must be running away from something and guessing his mind was in turmoil totally confused. He had been talking during his delirium about the emotional experience he had been through at the temple. It had seemed to them; he was running away out of frustration, and a feeling of impotence. They had talked among themselves, the possibility of offering to take Jesus with them when they resumed their travel home. However, because of his age would he not be better to return. They believed from his ramblings, here is a youth, frustrated and confused. Not just trying to find and understand his God, but grasping at what it was he believed. It seemed when looking at all of what he had just seen; he could live within the laws of his religion while still seeking a truth that so far had eluded him. They could understand his dilemma. If he travelled with them and learned how others found their way, he in turn might find his. On the other hand, was he ready for what he might discover. They shared these thoughts with Jesus, whatever he wished to do they were there to help.

They explained he was welcome, to travel with them, or they would help him find his way back to his home. Jesus took a deep breath, seeking answers inside of his mind, asking for Gods guidance. He looked at these two men and said; "I would be very grateful if I could accompany you. Then Jesus took a deep breath, and with a smile on his face, said; May I ask you a question please?" The monks chuckled a bit and said; "we think you are going to ask us many questions before we part company. Please go ahead." Jesus said; you told me you went to Jerusalem with your begging bowls." "Yes, that is right," they said.

"What is it you wish to know."

Jesus asked. "Whom did you ask for food, surely there are no Buddhists in Jerusalem. Everyone there is a Jew other than the cursed Romans of course."

The Buddhists looked at Jesus with a smile, and reaching out touched his hand. "No young master we had developed a Buddhist community several years ago, and it is growing. Also, you must know there are Gentiles there as well" Blushing Jesus had taken his second step toward a more open mind. The young Jew was on his way. To where he had no idea, but he 'would put his faith in these two men who had befriended him. He knew God was guiding him.

As they travelled along the roadway, they told Jesus how this prince, Siddhartha, left his father's palace one day, and for the first time saw people suffering, dying, and dead. People so poor they had no place to sleep or food to eat. He saw beggars sitting at the side of the road crying out for food. Living inside the palace grounds he never had an opportunity to see anything other than a life of plenty. He had no knowledge of this other side of life. The king, his father, had kept the knowledge of all types of suffering from him. Compassion and pity filled the prince's heart. He went back home pondering all of this. He thought of his future and then thought of those with no future. His destiny was to be a King someday. Since before his birth, his life had was planned. "Is this what I want for myself." He knew the answer was, No. Something inside was talking to him. There was more he could do. More he could learn. One night he quietly slipped away from his wife and child, from all the luxury of his home, and become an ascetic.

The story continued. The first few years proved to be difficult. Initially, the Prince followed a path of renunciation and strict fasting. That left him with little strength. He was unable to meditate properly. Then he adopted a mode of discipline, more of a middle path, which is more like we monks follow today, avoiding the extremes of self-denial, also self- indulgence. Years passed, he travelled with other monks, and sometimes alone, but always trying to find a way to avoid the suffering in this world. Finally, one day he found himself sitting under a large tree, with his eyes closed. He slowly began to meditate. Then with the help of his inner self was guided. Later he just "woke up." Now he knew and fully understood the cause of suffering. He could see that there was a way the endless suffering of this world, could come to a final cessation.

Jesus looked at these two holy men, seeing them as truly holy, for the first time. These were ordinary people, who had taken the mantle of, priests, rabbis, and teachers, but also humble men. He admired their sincerity and humbleness. In his mind, he compared them to Caiaphas. They were not Jews, but he knew God wrapped them in His love, no matter what their religion. He found himself chocked with emotion and was speaking in a whisper, but he asked; "Did Buddha accomplish what he set out to do?" "To answer your question briefly, yes. He did. Now it became necessary to travel over a large area preaching and gathering disciples with him as he went.

Jesus wondered; did God direct the Buddha to make the decision to become a monk? Does God, his God, influence other religions to do his work? There is only one God and that must be the God of Jerusalem. My God, our God, the Jewish God was also the God of all mankind>

# Chapter Eight

THE PATIENT WAS well enough to travel and the three of them set out. Jesus was feeling good. During the night, he slipped out of the tent and prayed. Asking God to tell him if he was doing the right thing and did his family understand. He woke up in the morning knowing all of this is what God would want from him. The road was dusty and the day hot, but a soft breeze made walking tolerable. Jesus seemed totally unaware of what was around him for the first hour of walking. He continued to mull over his present situation. The Jewish people believed in staying together. These people were Buddhist's. Was this the right thing to do? The young Hebrew asked that question to himself. How can travelling with people of another faith be wrong when the two monks were such good people? He answered the question himself. God answered the question while he slept. This is where I am supposed to be. God was his guide. He must trust and have faith.

    He was compelled by his desire to learn. Something within him was drawing him to the unknown like a moth to a flame. Back home, James instructions in religious matters did not fulfil his desire for knowledge. Something was lacking. Even the local rabbi, answering questions through

James, seemed to fall short of his expectations. Looking back now Jesus asked himself; "Who am I to question those who teach?" But he did. Every night and many times during the day, back in Nazareth he would quietly pray to God asking for guidance. This trip was God's answer. He had asked God answered. That resolved he straightened his shoulders and marched on.

The strangers were no longer strangers; they now had names. The monks made it easier for Jesus to pronounce their names. They became and Gur and Jit to Jesus. The three plodded on together, moving into the unknown, at least to Jesus.

Probably because of all the questions and forthcoming answers, Jesus was becoming a more open-minded person since leaving the temple. He realized there was a much larger world out there, and he had a great deal more to learn. Thinking back to his former community and their scorn of the Gentiles and the Romans. Does God look at them the same way? The priests and the rabbis scorned all who were not Jews. Is it up to us to judge? When the Pharisees despised other Jews, who they considered lower than themselves, does God feel likewise? While Jesus did not recognise it, he was beginning to change. Here, far away from home, he was beginning to think for himself, and he knew it. As he thought to himself, he chuckled out loud. His companions noticed and winked at each other.

As the three travelled together, Jesus got to know Gur and Jit better; he realized that the monks were real people, who dedicated their lives to helping others. Must God not love them also? He began to turn these thoughts over in his mind. Is it possible that one can still be a Jew and yet recognize the rights and beliefs of others, without spurning their teachings and beliefs? He was more open now to the concept that Jews were no better or worse than anyone else. You must belong to some tribe. He belonged to the Jews. But that didn't mean that he was any more chosen than any other peoples. That made him feel stronger and better. He carried his head higher as he walked, and breathed deeper, the air clearing his mind. At home, these thoughts would never enter his head or heart. He realized now that by leaving home he had opened himself up to experience a much larger world. Confidence rose in him like a river overflowing its banks. Jesus knew he had made the correct decision, and he was on his way to find answers. Could he teach this new knowledge back home? That would be a challenge.

There was another question bouncing around in his mind. Was the God of Israel only a Jewish God or was this God the one and only God of all people? Could it be when God said, you are my chosen people, the meaning was not exclusive to Jews? There was an answer to this question, but he admitted he did not have it now. He stumbled and almost fell as they continued along the trail. Tripping on small stones, because his mind was elsewhere, had become a common occurrence. The monks would look at him and smile, sensing and feeling the intensity of this young man. Or Jesus might throw up an arm, and suddenly stop in his track, as a new possibility entered his mind. When he did that, he would look sheepishly at his companions and grin.

Jesus was now beginning to understand Israel was only a small a part of the world. He also had concluded there is only one God. Of this, there was no doubt. Had he stayed back home, he would never have questioned these things. That was the reason God put him here on this path. More new experiences and new beliefs would open the way to total understanding. There might be danger ahead, but Jesus believed God was guiding him and protecting him. So many questions. The Torah warned God is a jealous God would punish those who worshipped other than him. Is there another way to interpret that? He was to find the answer to that in the next fourteen years.

He was likely to encounter knowledge that would challenge his belief as a Jew. However, while there might be challenges, what he had learned at his mother's knee was strong enough to help him to see the truth. In a short period, Jesus began to believe that no religion could claim the one and only God exclusively as theirs. His mind must remain open if he was to reach a higher understanding.

The three travellers talked of many things as the days passed and they continued their cross-country trek. They shared much of their individual pasts. Jesus told of his mother and father and his desire to know God. Jesus' recollections flowed effortlessly, such was the blessing of a young memory. On his part, he had a lot he wanted to ask them. However, one question seemed too sensitive. Jesus wanted to know about the Buddha and where he fitted into their beliefs. Finally, he broached his question. "Is the Buddha the God you worship?" The answer came quickly. "Buddha is not a God. Perhaps in his life, he had become a divine person. But we do not recognize just one God as you do. The Buddha had a mission. He wished all people to find wisdom, freedom, peace and mostly an end to all suffering. That he called Nirvana. Our Buddha left the world with four truths so all could reach Nirvana as he did." Jesus sat staring into the fire, "I need time to digest all of this," he told them with a little smile on his face, he was ready to retire for the night.

Several days had passed before that conversation came up again. Jesus enjoyed the daily travel, new vistas, green fields, or yellow fields of ripening grains. Red poppies bloomed in abundance along the well-travelled paths and along side creek beds. Stops here and there with people the monks knew. There were visits with followers who live in little communities along the way. Their modest houses made of red clay offered respite and shade from the midday sun. Jesus was impressed with their serenity and joy with which their followers expressed their gratitude. Their offerings of goods no matter how humble came with love from their hearts. It was given unselfishly; some of them reached out to touch their robes.

It was not surprising then that Jesus' questions kept coming. But, he did not wish to abuse the hospitality of his hosts. Thus, he held back if he could. Until finally he could not restrain himself. He was fit to bursting with curiosity. He remembered his brother James telling him to stop talking and just listen for a change. Here in the middle of this strange land, Jesus wanted only to listen. The Buddhist monks were very patient and very compassionate and had no trouble seeing what their fellow traveller wished to know. "We think you have a lot of questions, and we will attempt to answer all of them. One of the most important things we do, is to explain our way of life. We believe by living a good life while here on the earth, it will not be necessary to keep coming back again and again. As a Buddhist, our task is to live a life per the laws of our religion. Doing this will hopefully put a stop to the endless cycle of being born again and again, and subject to all kinds of hardships, trouble and misery."

Is this not what we attempt to do also, or am I missing something; Jesus mused?

The monks had no trouble seeing that Jesus was not understanding what they were telling him, it showed all over his face. "Do you have a question? If so, please ask." The young student finally said. "Coming back. I do not understand what you mean by coming back." Jesus remembered what it was the Buddha was trying to accomplish. He just did not know what is meant, by 'coming back." They had told him, "a way to help all people to refrain from coming back to earth again and again." It was called Nirvana. "When our soul leaves the body and we realize we did not accomplish what we had wished for while here on earth, we are unhappy with ourselves. Our soul goes back to where it came from. There we review our time on earth, and we must come back here in a new body to try again to finish what was left undone, or make over what we did wrong, in that life.

Think about this for a bit, see yourself as that soul and ask, did you, Jesus, come back this time, with the desire to learn and teach?"

Jesus was shocked. "I did not know I had come back.' This suggestion caught the young Jew by surprise. He was without words. Now suddenly 'coming back' was not something about some one else, but it was he who might have come back. Coming back; from where? Had he 'Jesus' done that? From where? Suddenly the thought had a new meaning. Had he Jesus the son of Mary and Joseph from the little community of Nazareth been here on earth before in another body? Another person, with another name? Neither his mother or James had ever talked of this. He needed time to cope with that question. The monk reached out and touched Jesus' arm and said. "You have so much you want to learn, kindly remember that full knowledge takes a long time and will not come in one day. Jesus thought of little else for the next week.

As it happened, the three travellers arrived at a village larger than any they had visited before. Here Jesus saw people who covered not just their heads, but their faces as well. He learned they were a group called Jains. Jesus asked about them. "You have enough to think about now. You can learn more about them later" was their reply.

It was inevitable Jesus would reopen the subject of souls coming back. Was this something only Buddhists believed. It was certain no one back in Nazareth had ever mentioned this to him. Yes, this is not Jewish. Jesus often thought about his religious training back in Nazareth. Because he and Thomas were outcasts in their community, we were excluded from studying and training with a Rabbi. They relied on James and their mother. There was so much he did not know about his beliefs. He acknowledged both his mother and brother James had tried to teach them, but here again, his impatience had likely deprived him of learning as much as he might. Do my people believe we come back again and again? I do not think so, we certainly never discussed that at home.

Jesus knew that when one died, they would go to heaven, to be with God the Father, providing they had lived per the law. Could there be more? It seemed to him that there was much more. Therefore, God has led me here. If I am to be one of Gods prophets, I have much to learn and I must know what I teach, it is what God wishes.

So, the day came when all three thought it was time to discuss those subjects left unanswered. "I have never been taught much about souls." Jesus started the conversation. "This is something new to me. I believe when one dies they go to heaven to be with God. I know I have a soul, all people do, but that is as far as it goes. How many people stop and think about their soul? If what you tell me is true, then we are our soul and not just a human body. When the human mind lives a life that is not in accordance with what we wanted to live here on earth, is it the soul who is punished? Are we that soul? There is so much I have taken for granted. I have missed much by not seeing the whole picture. I also have believed, since I was a child, we Jews are a chosen people, God will look after us. Now I wonder if chosen means what I had thought it to mean. I find it hard to disbelieve my teaching, and yet I cannot disbelieve what is in front of my eyes."

The one monk who went by the name Gur, short for Gurjeet, offered a response to Jesus' queries. Gur's skin was so smooth, and Jesus had begun to think of him as the monk with the shiny face. It was he who would usually speak first. "Yes, we are familiar with the Jewish belief in a God of Israel. That is something you must work out for yourself. We respect what you believe; it is possible that without contradicting your previous thoughts, you may find there is another way of understanding. As you travel this road, you will see many other ways of seeing the same subject. Let me tell you a story; Once three men were arguing about God. The first one said. 'God is the sun, see how it makes the plants grow. God is the Sun.' Another who watched a gentle rain give his fields water says, 'God is the rain, see how he gives drink to my crops.' While a third, who is tired, and needs rest, curls up on a large rock, warmed by the sun, said. 'You are both wrong, God is the wind, that blows the rain our way, and cools the heat of the sun. Only a God could do that." "You see my young friend there are many ways to solve the same puzzle. That is probably something you must work out for yourself."

Jesus pondered for awhile thinking. The Buddha looked for a way to stop the continuation of life after life. Must one be born again, only to die, and be reborn? Only to undo what was done, or what was not done in the past life? Is this what the Buddha dedicated his life to do?

God would have us live a life of love, charity, compassion, forgiveness, and trust, and in doing that, one would find a life eternal, after this life. We Jews believe that.

Was this also, not what the Buddha was teaching. Live by Gods plan, and you have eternal life? However, he held his thought to himself.

The monks continued. "The Buddha taught us life is impermanent; we call it no self." The second monk whose name was Efforts, added: "I bring this up to help you understand why we do not think this doctrine of suffering as pessimistic. It is realistic, to accept that the human personality, and in fact all reality is forever changing. Ask yourself are you the same person today as you were ten years ago, or will be ten years from now? If you look at it this way the cause of suffering is not the constant change but the human desire to hang on to material things, these material things are how we see ourselves; they are what we are. In traditional Buddhism, no self, means that there is no permanent identity to continue from one moment to the next. Here is an example: you might look at that stream flowing by, and think this is the same stream as it was a moment ago, but it is not. The water you looked at a moment ago, is gone and more has taken its place, only to pass as well. When you look at a candle, and the flame you look at seems constant, but it isn't. It is continuously replaced by burning. Our selves are like that. You change every minute. If everything changes, it is possible for everything to become new. By accepting the doctrine of suffering, it is possible to approach even the most difficult situations in life, with a sense of lightness and freedom. If a person realizes that, there is no permanent self; there is no longer any reason to be attached to all the things that bring someone back in the cycle of death and rebirth. Accepting this realization is enough to start unravelling the chain of causes that bind people to samsara, and get them moving toward nirvana. We respect your beliefs and do not wish to change them. Our philosophy is available to all, but we are a peaceful people and will only go where we are wanted."

"I also am peaceful," Jesus said. "I believe loving your neighbour is God's way. Some have waged wars to force others to their way of thinking. They have killed those who would not change their beliefs. That is not how I think, and would not be part of a religion that forces its beliefs on others. God gave all of us the right of free will. But wait I do have one more question," Jesus asked and then laughed as he continued, "Perhaps, I should say, another question, please. I often see you walking with your hands in prayer and chanting. Tell me about that."

"We are saying a mantra; it is a prayer, a form of meditation. The words are not as important as the feeling. We become those words, as we are saying them, we are living them; we are one with all of eternity. Another way of saying this is, the power of the phrase, resides in the syllables themselves, rather than in their meaning." Jesus was clearly puzzled.

"Listen to the sound of that water," the monk said as he pointed to the roaring stream beside them. "Allow all other thoughts to leave your mind, so your soul can move closer to God, you believe in one God, let this be the path to your God, let the sound of the water be your mantra. As you listen to the water, allow all other thoughts to leave your human mind, and feel God within you."

# Chapter Nine

THE TRIO WOULD often leave the beaten path to reach small Buddhist communities. Here the monks would heal, pray, and teach. The messages were not always in a language Jesus understood. One language that most often was used was Hindu which the monks were helping Jesus to learn. During these gatherings, Jesus would sit back of those gathered to observe and listen. Before the meeting, they would set up a small campsite, and bring out holy objects, for the people to handle. Occasionally, they would build a mound and place a small artifact inside. This will someday become a shrine or even a temple to honour The Buddha.

The monks would administer ointments to heal the sick and build cairns to honour the dead. At the same time, they would receive new members into the Buddhist family. Then after a feast and a good night's sleep, with much goodwill and fond farewells, they moved on. One such side trip, Gur, the monk with the shiny face, said, "The Buddha left us with many little thoughts, as well as his main messages. One of these I especially like; The Buddha said; "Words have their place, but one can convey a teaching through gestures, a smile, a tilt of the head, or even through silence. Buddhism is teaching the way to live a serene and contemplative life. One may teach as much by example as by words." Jesus believed this and promised himself to remember to follow these words.

Jesus knew his mission in life, was to teach the way of God. Accordingly, he listened intently, to everything these men taught him, in the hope that their words would broaden his understanding of God's will.

Later, looking back as he made his nightly talk with God, Jesus would tell Him how he could learn from these men who were of a different faith. Perhaps in some ways, their beliefs were different, but their intent was the same. He would say to God; they teach loving each other and practice charity wherever you can, once again this is what I believe.

Wherever he went, he met people who saw things differently, but when examined closely the religion of others seemed not as different after all. Yes, Jesus was growing not just physically, but more importantly spiritually. He was beginning to see the 'whole' picture. He had begun to see living in a small community where all believed the same would limit one's perspective. He could close his eyes at night honoured to know he had been chosen to view this revelation of cultures and religions.

The Buddhists, even though their beliefs were not the same never felt threatened by Jesus own religious dogma. Nor did they ever attempt to convert him to Buddhism. They, allowed him to blend his fundamental understanding with what he was learning, and take or reject it as he saw fit. Jesus no longer felt guilt when he learned someone else' point of view, but now understood there was often truth behind it. It was remarkable how these monks had become role models and they weren't even Jews.

One day, looking for place to stop and rest, they chose a campsite alongside a small stream which ran through a grove of trees. They gratefully sat putting their feet in the cool water. They chose this camping place because it provided delightful shade and fig trees still bearing a bit of fruit. All of them were happy to get out of the sun. It was very hot this day, as were most days, they were tired and in need of cool water to rinse off the dust of the trail, as well as enjoy a cool drink. Looking around, Jesus turned to his friends and said, this is a very nice place to stop, I'm truly ready for a rest. Years later, Jesus would reflect on that day and realize God had guided them to that spot. While he did not recognise the significance then, it turned out that oasis would lead to a change in his life.

As all three were bending over the water and splashing their faces, when they heard voices and little bells. They could hear the fall of animal's hooves, and creaking harness. Startled, they looked up and saw a caravan approaching from the direction they had just come. It turned out to be a trader heading back to India with goods from China and other parts of the Middle East. The men were a mixture of Indians and Arabs. They drove camels and donkeys, all laden with goods for markets up the road. Jesus arose from the ground for a closer look. Despite his new maturity, there were times when he was still an inquisitive boy. Fascinated with all he saw, eager to smell, see, and touch. Despite the heat and dust, this caravan brought a feeling of good cheer.

A strong young man, perhaps eight years older than Jesus, stopped and addressed them in Aramaic. "She lama, my friends may we camp alongside of you?" A large man, with broad shoulders and strong arms, he had fierce eyes, topped by heavy black eyebrows. This all added up to a bold look. His dress was white to reflect the hot sun, much as Jesus was clothed. Gur arose and walked over to greet the entourage. Perhaps the little group of Buddhists and Jesus, were not an important trio in the eyes of this man who was obviously the leader, but it turned out he treated them as such. He told them we too are travelers, and would welcome your company." Jesus was impressed with the size of the group, and while he could not know it at the time, he and the leader of the caravan, would become close friends. Jesus was to travel with him for years, to many different countries. Even as far away as China. The young Jew quickly rid himself of the selfish and strange feeling that suddenly overtook him. Chastising himself for this feeling. He realized it was the thought of a lost opportunity. He wanted to continue the learning experience he was enjoying with the Buddhists. Perhaps they too might add to his education.

Gur read the look of disappointment on the face of this young Jew, and instinctively knew what he was thinking. The wise old man, moved over to Jesus, and quietly whispered; "We will not lose our time together, but in the company of these people, we will be much safer on the road ahead."

The new group scattered among the fig trees, helping themselves to the fruit. Jesus looking at the trees, could not help but note how the unattended orchard could use the help of his brother Jude. That young man would have kept them pruned, and easier to harvest. Thoughts of home overtook him most days. It was at times like this, that deep feelings of emptiness would sweep over him. He so desperately wanted to be with his family. However, he knew there would be many more months, perhaps years ahead, until he understood, what it was he was being guided to learn.

It turned out this addition to their little group was going to take him closer to the truth he was seeking. Years later when reflecting on how his life had been guided, he would go back to this moment and in complete awe, wonder at the invisible hand that had always been there. When Jesus encountered these mixed feelings, he allowed himself to enter a part of his mind where he felt the closeness of God. This kept him on track by helping him push away those lonesome feelings and see the positive. With that mental adjustment, he never questioned his decisions. In fact, his reaching out and touching God, allowed himself to look forward to what might come next.

The monk thanked the leader for speaking Aramaic, He said their young friend was Jewish and could not speak Arabic. "I recognized him for a Jew immediately, and expected that to be the language of the day." He grinned as he said this, and added; "My name is Ishmael, what will I call you my friend?" "I am Gur, or Gurjeet. My fellow Buddhist here is Efforts, and the young man is called Jesus. As a traveller, I am sure you know Aramaic not Hebrew, is the language most commonly used by the Jews of Galilee, Judea, and Syria. Occasionally, Hebrew will be spoken at home usually on a feast day. We speak Aramaic to Jesus as it is the most comfortable language for him." Ishmael nodded and said, "We were in Jerusalem last year, and always spoke Aramaic."

Later, Jesus broke away from the rest of the group and walked among the fig trees where he could be alone. Humbly in the glow of a full moon he talked to God. Jesus was uncertain and did not completely know why. Perhaps it was just a feeling he had because of the arrival of Ishmael and his fellow travellers. He could not understand why, but he had an inner feeling his life was about to head into a new direction. He asked for help to understand what God wished him to do. There were several concerns he had lately. Was he allowing the monks to influence him into losing his own beliefs? Did the arrival of these new people interfere with what the monks had been teaching him? What new religious beliefs might he encounter in the next months that lie ahead? Sometimes the way others worship is so very different from what I have been taught. Other times I can see a similarity. I am here to learn. Yet often what I learn, challenges what I have been taught to believe since a little boy. Please help me to keep my mind open. As he talked to God, he saw a falling star seeming to race across the sky. It appeared to be heading in the direction Jesus and the monks had been travelling. As he looked he heard a soft voice speaking to him;

"Do not fear my son. You are going in the right direction and I am with you always."

Not far away another figure was on his knees also praying. Ishmael was asking the same God, in his own way, to keep everyone safe in this dangerous part of the world. Ishmael also heard a gentle voice telling him to take the young Jew under his care. The Arab was deeply moved.

The next morning it was agreed by everyone, Jesus and the monks would travel with the caravan. The monks would remain for what would become a little more than a month. After which they would reach their goal, and would leave the caravan. However, the Buddhist monks told Jesus they still had a lot of time to work with him.

During that period, Jesus and Ishmael would become friends. The two had agreed that Jesus become part of the caravan for an indefinite period. They would visit many countries, including far away China. Here Jesus would meet Buddhists whose beliefs were somewhat different than those of his friends. Jesus wondered why people who believed in the same Buddha, could see that leader through different eyes. He talked to God about it. Jesus asked himself, is this not the same with most people who worship God. Humans argue over the little things, when loving God and each other was all that mattered. He was to see many more examples of the differences during his travels.

Jesus asked Ishmael about China. It was the first time they had been there, Ishmael explained. They would be going back again much later. During that trip, he would take him up a mountain where he would meet a special order of Buddhists who claim to be the only real Buddhists. There would be times Jesus encountered religions whose Gods were earthly objects, such as animals, idols, or even the Sun and Moon. 'Have you seen any of this, Ishmael?' "Oh yes and you will too, my friend.

As they sat by fire in the bright moonlight. Jesus had been silent and then he spoke:

'Mankind was gifted with a brain. The brain is human, no other species on the planet had a mind with such freedom of choice. Be that choice good or bad, God has given humans a choice. It is that choice where the soul and the human should work together. How many times had people allowed the love they have for God, turn to hatred when encountering the convictions of others? Many times! Jesus suddenly spoke these thoughts aloud. The monks and Ishmael looked at each other and grinned. Continuing to talk to himself, he waved his arms and continued; "how many innocents have died and will continue to die because of these convictions?" The young Jew looked a bit sheepish as he realized he seemed to be preaching.

As they travelled, Jesus learned so much about the life of a trader. This business was not so much the buying and selling, it seemed the skill was in the trading. When they stopped in a town and sold some goods, instead of receiving coin, they took local goods, such as carpets, tea, or even jewellery. The locals, would argue the price attempting to buy it as cheaply as possible. Then often, slyly, would bring out their own products, whereupon a trade was arrived at. He was astounded when the Arabs would raise the price of their goods before meeting with merchants, knowing they would be forced to reduce it. Alternately, when buying, Ishmael and his men would argue for hours, even leaving, only to come back later to buy for as little as possible. Jesus, who had been raised in a barter system, and secretly believed money was evil, understood the barter part. However, back home, no one tried to make a profit when trading wheat for shoes for instance. These were your neighbours. He had always been aware of the power of greed, but he grudgingly admitted, while buying and selling was an important part of earning a living, he never for the entirety of his life was comfortable with currency. All because of the greed that grew from it. As his twin brother, I can attest that Jesus could be as obstinate as any person I have ever known. It was both his strength and his downfall. After he had arrived back home, some said he was mad, many saw him as a God, but he was neither, he loved everybody, and only wanted all to love, share, and see God as a way of life. What worked in Nazareth, would not necessarily work all over the world? Or could it?

One day before the monks departed they told Jesus this story.

"There was a man called Antheridia, who was a Ganapati, or donor, who purchased a property as a gift for the pleasure and use of the Buddha and his community of monks. He was a layperson just as the people the monks had visited that morning, and they, the monks, had received similar generosity. While generosity is not one of the five moral precepts it is a virtue. Among the other virtues, it allows the monks to live a monastic life."

"The lay people, have these five precepts: no killing, no stealing, no lying, no abuse of sex, and no drinking of intoxicants. We monks have those and more: We cannot eat after the noon hour, cannot sleep on soft beds, and cannot handle gold and silver. We engage in mental concentration, (Samadhi) which is to focus and clarify the mind, and we do prana, which is the understanding of no self. By following these principal's, we prepare our return in rebirth. The path to Nirvana is divided in eight categories, right understanding, right thought, right speech, right action, right livelihood, right effort, right mindfulness, and right concentration." Jesus looked impressed, and it showed. Efforts laughed, and told him, it seems like a lot, but we reduce these to three, moral conduct, mental concentration, and wisdom. That was their final example they had to leave with Jesus.

Saying goodbye to these two friends was difficult. They had travelled together for more than a year. Stopping at so many places, leaving the beaten path to travel to small villages, that the monks visit Buddhist communities. His months with them had been an education. That last lesson describing the principals of the lay people and the even greater duties of the monks, was a parting gift for Jesus. The young Jew was filled with wonder, at the tranquility and peace these good men brought with them, wherever they went. All three wept as they parted.

So, as he left one new friendship he began a new one as he became a member of a trading caravan. A new friendship was born. Jesus was to spend many years with these new friends. They travelled a far and wide. From China, they traded goods for tea and silks. Leaving behind carpets, woolens, and food products. It was here Jesus saw gold for the first time, along with jade. Then back to Syria and parts of Persia heading for India. During these trips, they would go to out of the way places, to obtain local products for sale elsewhere. As they walked side by side and continually talked, Ishmael and Jesus had long discussions about what Ishmael called the similarities between the beliefs of a Jew and those of many Arabs. Jesus could not help but see a few similarities between Buddhism and his own Jewish convictions, but he was eager to learn how what he had been taught could find similarities in the Arab mind.

# Chapter Ten

ONE DAY, JESUS and Ishmael were walking together when Jesus in his usual candor, reminded him about a comment he made regarding similarities in their religions. Ishmael, after a short hesitation replied, "We believe in the same God you do. Our history goes back to Abraham as yours does. I will tell you the story of Abraham and his wife Sarah as we see it.

'Abraham after reaching the age of eighty-six and his wife Sarah was still childless. This was a bitter disappointment to him. He so wanted a son, very much."

Jesus knew this story well, but remained silent.

Knowing how much Abraham wanted a son, Sarah suggested Abraham take her handmaiden Hagar as a possible surrogate mother. Abraham agreed and prayed to God for guidance in this decision. After many evenings, praying to God. Under the stars, on a hillside overlooking his home, Abraham finally knew God would approve. Therefore, Abraham took Hagar to his bed. She soon became pregnant. When Hagar conceived, she took great delight in the little one inside her, and continually talked about her pregnancy. So much so, it disturbed Sarah greatly, to the point she had a hard time keeping her jealousy under control. Despite the law and the custom stating, the baby would belong to Sarah.

Regardless, the resentment continued very openly. Finally, poor Hagar was unable to live with the hatred that now burned inside Sarah. So much so Hagar became desperate and was forced to flee the house."

With his eyes closed, as he reached back into his memory, Ishmael continued: "Hagar ran off into the wilderness where she sat contemplating her fate. Suddenly an angel appeared. Calming Hagar with good news. She was told she would have a son, and she should call him Ishmael. This will be no ordinary boy, the angel continued. He will be wild, and constantly in turmoil with others, never-the-less he will become a great leader whose descendants will be numerous."

The present Ishmael stopped, there on that well-worn trail and looked at Jesus out of the corner of his eye. He wished to see how his story was being absorbed. Obviously, Jesus was behaving in the appropriate manner, so the big man carried on. "Hagar liked what she heard, and returned to Abraham's house, where she delivered a boy which she called Ishmael." The present day, Ishmael stopped once more, only to look at Jesus with a small grin, and proudly pointed out, that he had been named after this child. Feeling good, seeing Jesus duly impressed, he began again.

"Abraham was eighty- seven years old when the boy was born, and very proud of this strong young son of his. He kept the boy with him constantly. Shortly after the birth, obeying God's wishes, Abraham called all his people around him to perform the circumcision ceremony. This son of Abraham, was all his father could have hoped for, and understandably they were close.

Then when Ishmael was almost thirteen years old, God called on Abraham and telling him, 'Sarah will become pregnant once more and give him another son.' Abraham was one hundred years old and Sarah ninety when this miracle happened. Abraham was jubilant and celebrated with a feast inviting everyone he knew. He went into the wilderness and made an offering by sacrificing a goat. Abraham spoke to the Lord once more during the sacrifice, asking about his boys. God promised him his two sons would become great leaders, both faithful to the Lord God. Then God added, the second child was to be called Isaac."

Jesus had a manner, everyone who knew him recognized, and this manner did not escape the eye of Ishmael. He noticed Jesus pursing his lips, as though he were holding back a question, yet not wishing to interrupt.

"Go ahead and ask it Jesus. I can tell you've something on your mind." Jesus hesitated for a minute or two, then finally, Jesus spoke up; "You are right my friend, there is a great similarity in your beliefs and mine. You do not call yourself a Jew, and yet you look like a Jew, and have many customs of a Jew,"

Ishmael hesitated, and a scowl slowly developed on his face. Jesus looked concerned fearing he had said something to insult his friend. Then a softer look slowly replaced the frown and the big man gave a great bellowing laugh. "Many of my people would kill you for saying we are like Jews, but I will receive it as a compliment." So, saying he stepped forward and gave the younger and smaller man a huge hug.

Now Ishmael was wound up and encouraged to continue. The Arab was not a man to speak more than necessary but here and with gusto he carried on. "When the child was born, Abraham called his first son to him. Placing his hands-on Ishmaels shoulders, the old man told him, he was to oversee teaching his little brother, and ordered the boy to keep the little one close to him. Isaac grew up following every footstep of his older brother, whom he idolized. This rough outdoor young man, had a quick temper, and was short on patience, which meant the youngest would and could receive a quick slap if he did not follow instruction. To all this Abraham heartily approved, but not Sarah. She resented this older boy, whom she saw as half animal, teaching her son. Sarah also resented his mother, who she called slave woman. She implored Abraham to send them both away. Sarah nagged constantly. Asking her husband to rid the household of the two slaves. This Abraham was loath to do. Ishmael was a fine young man, and a future great leader. Further, Abraham loved this first born, dearly.

One day, God called out again to Abraham, and said I wish you to sacrifice your eldest son, Ishmael to me. The stricken father could barely control his feelings. He so dearly loved this son, and the thought of sacrificing him dismayed him greatly. However, Abraham loved his God and respected his every wish. It was with great reluctance he took Ishmael up to the hills and prepared the sacrifice. At the last moment, God called out, and said Abraham sacrifice a goat, save Ishmael who will one day serve me as you do." The present-day Ishmael, looked deeply at Jesus and said, this proves to us God saw young Ishmael as a future leader and a great prophet.

Among us Arabs, there are a great number of tribes. Some of them worship other Gods, but we in my tribe, follow the descendants of Abraham and his son Ishmael.

Jesus had been tempted to intervene at one point. For according to Jewish belief, it was Isaac who was nearly sacrificed. This is what all Jews had been taught down through the ages. Unusual for him, but wisely, Jesus held his tongue. Neither man could possible know it, but another great prophet would arrive in about six hundred years and unite the Arabian tribes, acknowledging there to be only one God.

Ishmael's voice was giving out. He paused long enough to drink some water from his goatskin to relieve his voice.

Offering a drink to Jesus, who declined, he continued. "I spend too much time walking alongside my camels, not talking as much as I am doing now." After a few deep breaths, he resumed the story. "Sarah would not relent in her determination to rid her home of Hagar and her son. Abraham finally relented, and planned the best way to provide for mother and son in the open space of the wilderness. Before making any decision, he asked the Lord to bless his two sons. When the Lord blessed Isaac, Abraham asked for a blessing for Ishmael also, and the Lord said I have heard thee. I will make him fruitful, he shall multiply, and have twelve princes and become a great nation. They will live in the east of their brothers the descendants of Isaac. As I have already told you Ishmael will be known as the wild man. He will have many men against him but will triumph."

"Then Abraham returned home and asked the mother and son to leave, giving them as much food and water as they could carry. He supplied them with two donkeys and a pair of goats. They headed out into the Paran desert, where they wandered for days soon losing their way. One day finding a cool clear stream with shady trees all around they stopped and set up camp.

Here, tired, discouraged, and not a little afraid, Hagar sat with her son and wept. She felt so alone and so lost. Her son hearing his mother's anguish wept also. As they sat together in this little oasis, an angel appeared in a great light. This messenger of God, admonished her. Saying to them, why do you cry Hagar, did I not lead you to water? God hears you and promises to make this a great nation. Make your home here, and you will soon be joined by others and become a nation.

As he grew, Ishmael became a great archer, and used this skill to fight off other tribes who would seek to take their land. As prophesized, he married and had twelve male children and a daughter who grew up to marry Esau. My personal lineage extends back to a son of Ishmael's son of Hagar and Abraham. Our family is known throughout this land. It is this knowledge that keeps us safe as we travel the trading routes.

Jesus asked Ishmael if this story is exactly the way it had been told from generation to generation. Ishmael drew himself up to his full height and fixed Jesus with a stern look, "Exactly, word for word. That is the only way we will know who we are and where we came from." The tight little smile he bestowed on Jesus left little doubt his question had been answered honestly.

As the weeks and years passed, Jesus hair grew long, as did his beard. He developed from a boy to a man. His voice became the voice of the teacher he was to become. Travelling through many countries, visiting many races and cultures. Each with their own customs and beliefs. Meeting people who worshiped idols, the sun and the moon as well animals only helped to broaden his outlook. There were so many people he met too poor to feed themselves properly. They were forced to slave to make others rich. His resolve to champion the underdog, and speak out against greed became stronger.

One trip while travelling in China. Ishmael suggested they leave the caravan while it stopped to rest the animals. They suggested they take a short side trip. "You have spent time with the Buddhists," Ishmael explained; "But, here are more believers of the same religion. At the same time, different. I know Buddhism began in India, but when you meet these people, you may think this is where it all began. Or they may suggest it to you." He said with a wink.

It was a longer journey than Jesus had anticipated. They crossed a river and climbed a mountain trail. Eventually coming across several monks working in gardens. Despite the cold air at this height, the workers had pulled their robes down to the waist, leaving their upper body bare. Walking on and leaving these men behind them, the two came across a group of small buildings that looked like living quarters. Passing these they could see a trail winding up the mountain. There in the distance was a shrine or temple.

As they moved higher, an entire community seemed to be alive with people. Moving out of the group, and coming to meet them was a person such as Jesus had never seen before. He had met many old people, but never one like as this. The monk, looked as though he could be about one-hundred and fifty years old. (As it turned out he was.) However, he walked with the agility of a much younger man. On the other hand, his weather-beaten face was covered with a mass of lines, or wrinkles, which as Jesus noted, also covered most of the body not hidden under a brightly coloured robe. He looked so thin, it suggested he never ate food. His eyes, sunken far back in his head, seemed to be looking at Jesus with such an intensity he could feel them. The man behind those eyes turned out to be the head monk. When he addressed the two men, he spoke in a language Jesus did not understand, but apparently Ishmael did. After a brief exchange of words, the old man spoke to Jesus in his own language.

Up here in this very high mountain, the air was so cold, Jesus could not keep from shivering. Seeing the temple was much farther up Jesus was quick to ask, "Who would attend that place of worship which is so far away?" The answer was quick in coming. "This is a training school for young monks. They live here until they are fully trained, and then sent out to carry their message throughout the land. While the students take lessons up above, they also work the land and live in the cottages you have passed. The older monks, who do the training live in caves, underneath the temple."

They stayed here for three days. Sleeping under the temple, on benches of stone. Due to the incredible cold, Jesus and Ishmael slept under yak skins. They learned, the monks used no covering. During their stay, they met and lived with some of the oldest monks Jesus had ever known. This was Tibet, a land that seemed to be part of the sky. Ishmael and Jesus learned many of these people were over one-hundred years old, yet they walked spritely on some trails that took them even further up the mountain. Pathways cut out of stone one would expect to see only mountain goats travelling. Their diet consisted of some meat, vegetables, yak milk and a berry that is peculiar to the region. Jesus remembered that Gur and Effors consumed very little meat. Perhaps, because they lived mostly on the contributions of the faithful, there was little meat to be had. They maintained that these berries contributed much to their long life. Also, walking from the training area where the students were, up to the place of worship, kept them nimble and strong.

One day stopping for some tea and food, Jesus told them of the first two monks he had met and how much he had learned from them. He explained how they had saved his life. When they said their goodbyes, and were on their way back to the caravan, Ishmael asked Jesus for his thoughts or impressions. Jesus said, "Since I have been with you I have witnessed many ways to worship God, and some deity's seen as a God, but the Buddhists are unique, they do not have armies or weapons of war. They do not invade small counties and hold them hostage. They help the poor and homeless. They are good people. I could not become a Buddhist because I worship one God, while they believe there are more than one, or that is my interpretation of what they have told me. Yet I admire them and believe God smiles upon them. Buddhists love the land and its inhabitants, help others.

# Chapter Eleven

THE CARAVAN LEFT China and headed back home. After months of travel, with their cargo changing constantly, they finally crossed into what is now India. For some reason, Jesus felt a sense of excitement, anticipation perhaps. When his curiosity allowed his mind to ask God if something was about to happen, he had the strange sensation God was chuckling. No, he told himself, I just feel it is about time I went in a new direction.

His intuition was not wrong. Unknown to Jesus, Ishmael had made plans for Jesus to receive tutelage that would help the younger man's quest for knowledge. This had been done without Jesus suspecting. Ishmael was embarrassed lest his friend think he was trying to be rid of him. However, this would be an exceptional opportunity. Ishmael was confident this was an opportunity for his friend to find answers he had never had before.

It was time to tell him. So, this day as they were walking side by side, he decided now was the moment. He had been glancing at Jesus, getting up the nerve to break his announcement. Ishmael was more distraught than he thought he would be. Jesus on the other hand had noticed Ishmael's distraction, but decided to say nothing. When the trader was ready, whatever he had on his mind would erupt. That was his way.

Looking around Jesus had been aware the countryside seemed greener, the vegetation richer. This was new territory! Jesus mentioned this to his companion, commenting on the scenery, but his friend appeared to be thinking about something else, and seemed not to hear. Then Ishmael cleared his throat and cleared it again. Finally, whatever he was going to say, now was the time. He pulled his friend aside, reached out and took his arm. Jesus could not help a little smile. This was so unlike this bear like man. Then the words gushed out. "Jesus, I have made arrangements for you to spend some time with an ancient scholar. I use the word ancient correctly because he is old, very old, but his knowledge goes back a long way. This land we are entering is itself old, some think this is where the very first human was born. I don't know about that, but this teacher I am bringing you to has studied all the religion's this country has endured for centuries back. I asked my brother to make the necessary arrangements when he was here the last time."

"I hope you do not mind my friend." He seemed embarrassed. He squeezed Jesus arm and looked at him with concern. "I know I did all of this without consulting you, but I honestly believe you will learn more studying here with this man than you will travelling all over the world with me. I want you to know I am not trying to be rid of you. I love you like a brother, but you have a mission, you said so yourself, and this could be the best thing I could do for a brother and a friend."

Before hearing any of the details, Jesus knew whatever Ishmael had done was meant to be. It was part of the guidance that had brought him this far. Here was a continuation of Gods plan that had been part of his life since he left Jerusalem.

It was an answer to the prayer he had made to God, back at the temple.

Ishmael continued, "Jesus I hope you know you are welcome to travel with us for as long as you wish, but I also know of your desire to learn. Under the tutelage of this man you will acquire much of the information you seek. Since we met you have seen many lands and many cultures, but here in this land there is a different heartbeat. The pulse of this land is more vibrant. It is as I said; mankind might have originated here. You will learn so much. And you will love this teacher.

This was the reason for the feeling of something new. He had had it for days. The sense of anticipation and excitement grabbed him like two hands on his shoulders. He felt the might of God and the encouragement of his love. Oh, no doubt the hand of God was at work here.

Many years later when Jesus and I were once more reunited, he told me he was constantly amazed at the way his life seemed to be organized without his participation. Back then it was that feeling of spiritual guidance that kept his trust positive. Even when he had no idea what was ahead. (Thomas.)

They were entering what is now Pakistan. While Jesus had no idea where he was, or where the caravan was going, it soon would change direction again, and head south into India. The country then, was ruled by the Indo Greeks under King Strato. The caravan would travel many more weeks, stopping now and then to conduct normal business, until it reached the town of Ujjeni. Here Ishmael stopped, and turning to Jesus, said; "This is the end of the trail for you my friend." Jesus had a sinking feeling, but just for a second. He turned to Ishmael and with tears in his eyes, said; I am both thrilled, excited and sad. Please know, I cannot wait to meet this new teacher. Ishmael, I am so very grateful". The bond between the two had grown so strong, the parting was going to be difficult. Ishmael was the first close friend Jesus had ever had outside of his family. He was torn between the exciting future and the difficult separation.

When the animals and crew stopped for a rest and food, Ishmael had an opportunity to take Jesus down a roadway into this very ancient town. They walked until they could see an old stone building just up ahead. As old as the building appeared, it was not as old as the man who stood in the doorway appeared to be. That person looked up quickly. Probably he had seen them as they rounded the corner and was awaiting them. His face was lined with many wrinkles, long white hair hung to his shoulders. This was matched by an equally long white beard. Not to be outdone, shaggy white eyebrows shaded a banana shaped nose. He was small and thin, but his voice when he spoke was strong and surprisingly deep for such a diminutive person.

As he stepped forward to greet them, Jesus noticed him shuffled along, almost like a glide. Later he was to discover there was nothing wrong with his legs or feet. His sandals were much too large, and constantly falling off. Ishmael introduced him as Vishnu. Jesus stepped forward to greet him and was surprised to see the bluest eyes he had ever seen. His first thought as they met; 'person does not miss a thing.' Jesus bit back a little chuckle.

Vishnu quickly asked them in for a cup of tea. Inside a pot of water was boiling over a small fire. It appeared they must have been expected; yet, how could he possibly have known they would arrive just when they did? Jesus was to learn the elderly man always knew what was going to happen next. As Vishnu slowly moved to make the tea, Jesus was to learn nothing ever rushed Vishnu. Jesus who impatient by nature, was to learn life was going to move at the scholar's pace. The teacher graciously asked them to take seats on cushions spread about the floor. When the tea was served, Ishmael commented on the flavour. Being a trader who brought teas to this area from afar, he was quick to praise the quality and flavour of the brew. "It is excellent." Ishmael said somewhat surprised. He asked where it was grown. His surprise was evident to learn it came from right near the town they were in. An uncomfortable grunt was Ishmael s only response. Importing teas from afar and finding such excellence here was surprising.

A lull in the conversation gave Ishmael an opportunity to arise and embraced Jesus, and give a quick almost gruff good bye. Jesus thanked his friend profusely, telling him how sad he was to see him go. Emotional farewells were not Ishmael's strong point. He thanked Vishnu, asking him to look after this special friend and was about to take a quick leave, when Vishnu touched his arm and told him; "before you leave I want to tell you I am happy to have this new student and do have accommodation for him here in my home, as you requested. This will be my only student, just as you requested." Sensing Ishmael's desire to leave he quickly added. "I hope Jesus will have a long and profitable stay here." With that the big man took his hasty departure, but not before both Vishnu and Jesus noted tears in his eyes.

Vishnu now took both of Jesus hands, smiled at him hoping to comfort what he perceived as a nervous young man. He told him they would travel together over much of the countryside. That will be your class room. While this conversation was in Aramaic, Vishnu asked Jesus if he could speak Sanskrit. Hearing no, the old man said he would not only teach him to speak the language, but also to read and write it. Jesus asked if it would be possible to learn to read and write Aramaic as well. I shall be happy to do that also, was his answer.

As Jesus looked at the man who was to be his teacher, he could not help but admire once again the intense blue of his eyes, and how they seemed to be ringed with humour. The old man had such a happy look. As he got to know him better he found Vishnu enjoyed every moment of every day. He disliked no one, and found love in everything and everybody. Vishnu was overflowing with compassion and good will. The old man caught Jesus looking him and with a smile on his face said; "Are you scrutinizing me to see if I am real. Do you see me as an oddity?" Jesus was immediately embarrassed. "Master, please forgive me, you just look to be so happy and pleased with life, I could not help but admire that about you."

"I am happy," he replied with a sincerity that was very convincing, "I suppose, it is because I am content, I have food to eat, a place to live and clothes to cover me. When one is content and not constantly wanting, that person lives in love. Now that I have an opportunity to help someone my contentment is greater." Suddenly the loneliness Jesus felt at the departure of his friend was replaced by his own contentment. This caused him to wonder if this ancient man was human or an angel sent by God to help him. No, he mused, as the thought continued, there is little doubt he is flesh and blood. Perhaps he is an earth angel. God has many of those scattered around. Jesus had learned from Ishmael his tutor was one hundred and thirty-five years old, and judging from what he saw there were more years left in his small body. That certainly made him exceptional, even for an earth angel. Grinning Jesus put his arm around Vishnu's shoulder and said, "I do believe it will be easy to learn from you master. It is always easier to remember what one has been taught, when the teacher is happy. Because, when you are happy I will be happy too.

Later that day as the two were walking about the neighbourhood, Jesus stopped and looked at him, "You seem to be in such good health for a man of your years, do you have a secret?" "I think I do," Vishnu replied. "Each day I put twelve drops from a plant called sumac in my morning tea and have been doing so since I was a boy. That might be the reason." He chuckled in what seemed a cackle.

Vishnu went on to explain, "As my only student, we will be free to travel around, visit people of other faiths, such as Hindu, Buddhist, and learn something of Jainism. We will see them on their own ground practising what they believe and teach. You will see where they practice, and what it is they would have you know." Jesus told Vishnu of his time with the Buddhist monks, and of his visit to the mountain near China, but hastened to add he was sure there was much more to learn. During this conversation, they were wandering about the little town talking to many of the locals. It was evident this old man was held in high respect. Many asking his advice on a great number of matters. The student was impressed.

# Chapter Twelve

VISHNU BEGAN THE first day of teaching with an explanation of one of the main religious beliefs in his country. "We call it our sanatana dharama, this means eternal religion. There have been many changes to our beliefs. Being a Jew, whose religion has been steadfast through many years, you must wonder. I will explain why. We have been subjected to occupation by other countries, who conquered us to gain access to our spices, ivory, or natural resources. Mostly just to find land and plenty of water. We have both. When they marched in with their soldiers and elephants. They told us they were here to offer us protection. Unfortunately, we needed protection against them. Along with their troops, they also brought their religion. There have been many so-called protectors. Thus, we have worshipped Gods who are human, animals, stones, as well as the sun and the moon. As these conquerors come and go we add and subtract gods from our worship. One constant we have kept is the belief we should be grateful and say thank you daily. Does it matter if we say thank you to the moon, or the sun, if we understand there is a God who looks after us, and we tell him or her thank you. I believe there is only one God, so would it not be possible that God is the sun, the, moon, or and even an idol?"

"Do you not think a divine power has not the intelligence to see we are grateful, and loving, no matter where we find him? Why would a loving person hate someone who sees God differently, as long as they see God?"

Jesus needed to sit back and think. Vishnu stopped talking to allow this to sink into his pupil. In the mind of Jesus, he was remembering the holy words, I am a jealous God, and you shall have no other Gods but me. He quietly asked what am I to think God? If I were to see you in a stone or an idol would you be offended? Then the words came into his head clear and strong. 'There is but one God and that God is everywhere in everything including humans. You have me within you and so do all people everywhere. I love all equally, and forgive equally, no matter what they believe. No one religion is exclusive or excluded. Jesus heard and once more his mind was opening to a broader understanding of belief. Vishnu noted Jesus' mind was elsewhere for a moment and knew he was talking to God and God was talking to Jesus. He politely sat quietly and waited.

Vishnu asked Jesus. "What did you hear young man? Did not God just speak to you?" Jesus was aghast. "Do you see into my mind master?" The old man looked at Jesus with love in his eyes. "Sometimes when God wants it to be, so it is." Jesus continued to stare at Vishnu in disbelief. Perhaps this man is truly an earth angel. "I have sometimes felt you are more angel than human, master."

"What does it matter what I am, or what you are, if we accomplish what we wish to accomplish? Therefore, what does it matter where we find God? If in the end, we have learned to love and share and forgive, do you not think God will embrace us here on earth and keep us until we return to where we came from?" The old man laughed and wheezed and then went into a coughing spell until Jesus felt great concern for him. "Are you all right my dear friend?" Jesus leaned forward greatly concerned. Vishnu sat back, his eyes filled with tears from the effort, replied. "Yes, until I have done what I must do, and you are safely on the way back home nothing harmful will befall me."

Vishnu then continued as though nothing had happened saying, "Getting back to what has been part of what we believe, the four holy sites of Buddha are near here, and we have accepted many of his teachings and incorporated them into our beliefs. Keeping our minds open is one of our greatest strengths. Then allowing God to guide us when we are in doubt will keep us safe. Jesus sat and listened carefully. It was going to be necessary to pay attention.

"Many years ago, a civilization invaded us settling by the Sindhu (Indus) River. They were a well-organized people, sanitary, clever, and very artistic. Even though they were invaders, they did much for our country, building roadways, well-constructed buildings, enclosed sewage drains, and more important to us kept the peace. Along with all of that, they introduced their idols, which once again, we accepted in our easy manner. They lived among us a long time. Until another invader called Aryans moved in and introduced us to Veda, which has stayed with us. I want you to learn more about Veda, because it is a large part of what we believe. Veda is our religion today.

We use mantras in four Vedic Samhistas, (collections) which are compiled in Sanskrit. They are the Rig-Veda, the Yajur-Veda, the Sama-Veda, and Atharva-Vega. The Rig-Vega are mantras sung and practised from generation to generation as are all the Veda. This is so they will never be forgotten. That began two thousand years ago,

Rig means praise. We believe the hymns of the Rig-Veda and all Vedic hymns were divinely revealed to the Rishis, who were seers or bearers of the Veda, rather than authors. The Vedas are apaurashaya, this means uncreated by man.

Being from the Gods guarantees their unchanging status. Sometimes we worship elements such as fire and rivers, also there is the god Indra who has lost many followers, but she still gives me much comfort.

Days became months and months soon became a year. Jesus finally had learned to write and read Aramaic as well as Sanskrit. He had changed a great deal. Both in appearance and understanding. While he still considered himself a Jew, his acceptance of other beliefs as something recognized by God, had become easier to accept. All who sincerely say thank you, to whatever their concept of God, love others, are compassionate, and charitable, truly they have found the one and only God. Thinking back to his years in Nazareth, he had come a long way.

One day seeing Jesus was restless, Vishnu suggested a change. "There is a large community of Jews who live not far from here, would you like to meet some of your countrymen? The look on Jesus face was answer enough. Excited, he agreed willingly. Vishnu explained further, "these people fled Roman rule, and eventually found their way here. I believe you will find them as exited to meet you, as you are to meet them."

The two of them set off walking. Vishnu took Jesus to a different part of the town. One Jesus had never seen before.

On the way Jesus saw a small gathering of people who seemed excited, obviously enjoying themselves. Seeing this and looking for some excitement himself, Jesus wondered what was happening. Very curious he hurried over. Without thinking, he left his old instructor behind. Arriving there, well ahead of Vishnu, extremely curious he pushed himself into the gathering. The crowd being good natured moved aside for this stranger. Vishnu finally caught up and worriedly pushed himself into the gathering, to take a place beside his student.

Together they watched as a man walked on live coals in his bare feet, upon reaching the end, turned around, and walked back. The entertainer stepped off the coals turned to the crowd, with a smile of triumph on his face. As a further surprise, Jesus saw the entertainer had sharpened sticks protruding from his lips and other parts of his body. He then pulled the sticks from his face, strangely enough there was no blood. Jesus had never viewed this type of performance back home, so he watched fascinated. He could not understand why anyone would wish to hurt themselves.

The performer seeing a stranger in the crowd and walked over to Jesus to speak to him. Vishnu quickly whispered, "He normally speaks in Persian, but you may talk to him in Sanskrit, which he also speaks." The young man said, "My name is Arjuna, I see you are one who has lived on this earth before. I believe you are a holy man. You appear to be a stranger. Should you have questions, I would be pleased to answer them? He spoke in Sanskrit without being told to do so. Jesus replied, "How do you bear the pain, also how do you keep from injuring your self?"

"My mind controls my body, and tells it there is no pain, and no blood shall issue forth. My higher mind overrides my human mind. You are here to help the helpless. Is that not so?" Jesus did not reply but would never forget the conversation.

Continuing their walk, they passed through a very poor part of the town. Here Jesus saw huts made from branches, grass, or anything that could be used for shelter. The huts looked endless. Row after row, as far as he could see. People dressed in rags, bodies just skin and bone. Many deformed. They begged in a language unknown to him. This was the first time he had seen poverty such as this. Jesus found himself holding his breath, forgetting to breath, such was his sorrow for these people. His heart wept for them. Silently he lashed out at the inequity of life. This is not the way God wishes mankind to treat each other. Then he remembered the story of Buddha and his reaction in a similar situation. He understood a little better, why the Buddha did as he did.

As he stood transfixed, gazing at this small city of beggars, a small girl approached him. Standing at his side, she looked up into his eyes. She was so thin and obviously a beggar, her clothes hanging in rags. When his gaze took in her legs, they looked as though she had been whipped. Her hair was matted and dirty. She stared up at him as though he might not be real. Finally, putting aside her fear, she reached out and touched him. Looking down at her, he noticed for the first time; her face had the same deformity as his sister Ruth. His mind flashed back to his sister, and suddenly he was overwhelmed. Partly because of Ruth, but mostly for this tiny child. Emotion, love, and compassion flooded over him. Unconsciously he reached out, took both of her hands and said; in the name of God, let her be whole as God intended. With that he passed his hand across the child's face, and as his hand moved away, all who watched saw her features take on a look of pure beauty, the deformity completely gone. While the little girl did not know a change had taken place, those standing by most certainly did. Jesus held his hands together over his mouth looked upward and thanked God.

Vishnu quickly grabbed him by the arm. Silently, urgently he said; we must leave here now, or you will be in grave danger. For the first-time Jesus saw the reaction in the crowd as they began to move toward him shouting trying to touch him. Teacher and student fled.

They hurried down narrow alley ways and here found a busy street filled with shops. Vishnu stopped and held Jesus back said; "You have done more than heal her features. She has been used as a beggar girl and treated cruelly. Now she will be holy and respected by all as someone special. Her life will change decidedly, for she will be honoured. When she has grown to womanhood, she will be a leader for the very poor. Jesus said; 'but I did not heal the girl, it was God who did the healing.' Vishnu took Jesus by the arm and said; "No Jesus, you healed her in the name of God. Because of your sincerity and love the power of God was manifested in you."

They continued hurrying along as fast as Vishnu's old legs would go. Now excited and almost pulling his teacher, Jesus began to see many Hebrew symbols and lettering, some of which were in Aramaic. It did not occur to him he now could read, until he found himself understanding the signs before him. He stopped and said, "if I did not know better, I would think I was in Jerusalem."

Vishnu could not hold back the smile on his face, as he said, "We call this little Israel. There are many people here who came from your part of the world and would like to meet you. As he spoke, he pulled Jesus' arm and stopped in front of a stall, just as a merchant came out to meet them. It was obvious this man was a Jew. Emotion suddenly overwhelmed Jesus. It had been a long time since that day he ran away. How he longed for his countrymen and their way of life. The young student could not hold back his tears of joy. It was almost time for the feast of Passover, and Jesus had not celebrated any holiday since fleeing Jerusalem, all those many years ago, He had prayed to God for forgiveness, every time he was unable to take part in a Holy day.

As they introduced themselves, more Jews came from their shops. To join the little crowd. Vishnu made the introductions and explained the presence of his student. These fellow Jews were as excited as Jesus, and not about to allow this new country man to leave too soon. They asked Vishnu to allow Jesus to stay with them until after Passover. The elderly scholar agreed and promised to come back to pick him up when the holy days were over.

# Chapter Thirteen

OF COURSE, THE wonderful days in 'little Israel' had to come to an end. It had been good for him to have had this time with others whose lives like his, were steeped in Jewish tradition. The roots go deep. It is more than tradition that binds the Jewish people together. It is the love of God. The unwavering thread that goes back to Abraham himself. This is what Jesus missed. It is what he set aside to follow his burning desire to seek the true meaning of living a human life along with the wishes of God.

As agreed Vishnu arrived to pick him up for the walk back home. Jesus had a question to ask his instructor. One that had been on his mind since their visit to the man who walked on coals. "Master when I was talking to the man who walked on fire, he whispered in my ear; You have been here before, and now you are back to help the helpless. How did this total stranger know not only who I was, but who I might become?' Vishnu did not respond, but sat quietly waiting for Jesus to carry on. He knew there would be more. "Was I here before? What does that mean?" Vishnu smiled, for he knew this subject would come up. They had been talking around it for some time. The answer was part of what this young man needed to learn.

"Yes, I believe you were here before, and now have come back. Remember the Buddha and the task he gave himself? He saw so much suffering and felt most of it was needless. He looked for a way by which all souls might live right, and not need to come back to try to redeem themselves. Find a way they could love each other, as they love themselves, help the needy, seek a way in which all could live correctly and never need come back to this earth only to do it all over again."

Watching Jesus, to be sure he was understood, he continued. "We are all two parts and at the same time one. We came to earth as a soul to live in a human body with a human mind. The perfect way is both human and soul, live as God would have us do. In other words, live as one. We would share our wealth with the less fortunate; and love each other as we love ourselves. As you do now. You constantly keep God in your life. Some of us allow the human ego to take over and shove the soul aside to live a life of greed and selfishness. They forget the poor, even using them as slaves in their search for more human possessions. Greed has replaced God, and greed has robbed the soul of its original intentions here on earth. The soul has lost control, or decided to live as a human. When this happens, the soul, must come back to live as a human once more. Sometimes, a soul who has lived a good life as a human might need not come back, but may wish to return once more to do Gods work on this planet.

"Teacher if I was here before does that mean I failed in my last life?"

"Not necessarily, there are some God chooses to send back to help those who struggle. Prophets, and healers, teachers and even some who choose to come back maimed and poor. The latter to live among the more fortunate giving them an opportunity to help those who cannot help themselves. To be an example you might say. Some will die as martyrs to bring attention to the disorder mankind has created. I believe you are a chosen one.

Later Jesus sat and thought about what he had just learned, and strove to understand how and what he would teach, should he be a chosen one.

Did God give Moses the key to living the perfect life when he gave him the Ten Commandments? Was he a pattern to live life by? Perhaps God will bring back some souls over and over whenever the earth needs guidance. Could he, Jesus be one of those?

How many humans really understand their own soul? Or even know they have one and in doing so lose contact with God?

God lives in all of us. So, look within. Live as you had planned to live before you were born.

During a later session, Vishnu said, "Today I will introduce you to another religion of this country. These are others who believe in reincarnation. This religion is called Jainism, and in several ways, you will find much of what they believe to your liking. For these people are a peaceful society. They never make war. Jain Dharma is an ancient religion, and may be found here in this country just as you will find Hinduism and Buddhism. These people prescribe a path of peace and non-violence toward all living beings. The philosophy and practice depend much on self-effort in the progress of the soul on the spiritual ladder to divine consciousness. Any soul which has conquered its own demons, and achieved the state of a spiritual advanced being, is called jina. This means conqueror or victor. Jains are a very literate group. Their insistence on scholarship goes back a thousand years. Jains regard every living soul as potentially divine. Is this not a message for all humans? We come to this earth from a place of perfection, to seek divinity in a human form. Thus, to return having accomplished what we came for. How many humans work at self-effort, non-violence, love of neighbour as well as love of God, recognizing their soul as who they really are? I wanted you to learn something about the Jain Dharma, even though you may not be able to accept their entire philosophy, it seems there is something in all beliefs that lead one toward God."

"Because each Jain is encouraged to rely on their self for spiritual development and cultivate their own personal wisdom and self-control, that goal is buried deep within. Therefore, dedicated to saving their own souls, they take on the responsibility of their own salvation. The goal of Jainism is to realize the soul's true nature. These are the triple gems of Jainism. This they call moksha. Moksha provides the path for attaining liberation from samsara, the cycle of birth and death. Does that sound familiar? Those who have attained Moksha, are considered liberated souls which they call siddha."

"Those who remain attached to worldly possessions are called mundane souls.

Dull people whose God is money."

Vishnu stopped for breath and looked at Jesus closely to see if he had a better understanding of life after life and why some must be born again.

Jesus did have a much better understanding, and was thinking about each persons' connection to God, and to each other. Looking back at what he now knew about the beliefs of these people, the Buddhists, the Hindus, and now the Jains, he could see God working within what each believed. God loves all equally, and no matter how each one reaches out to God, it matters most how we treat each other, for God is in each of us. When we love, each other we are in fact worshipping God. God is love. That is where you find him. Without love, there is no God.

Praying without sincerity is not praying, it is only lip service, in which there is no love. To memorize a prayer and say it without thinking is not praying. Even a mantra must be said with thought.

"One more thing Jesus, The Jains believe that the Universe and Dharma are eternal, without beginning or end. The Universe undergoes processes of cyclical change. This same Universe consists of living beings and non-living beings. All worldly relations of living beings with other living beings and non-living beings are based on the accumulation of Karma and its conscious thoughts, speech and actions carried out in its current form.

There is a lot of emphasis on consequences of not just your physical form... but on what you think. Thoughts are a form of life. Thoughts are energy and carry an unspoken message.

There was much to think about, and Jesus knew his own thoughts had changed much since he left home. If God wanted him to take what he had learned, and tell it to all who would listen, there was much here that would offend the priests and rabbis back home. Jesus liked the non-violence, and the path of peace toward all living beings. Striving to climb the ladder to a divine consciousness, was what all people should be doing. It was a matter of fundamental knowledge the clear majority would not take on this personal task. Conquering one's own inner demons meant conquering anger, hatred, lack of charity, sexual habits out of control, jealousy, killing and greed.

'To regard every human as potentially divine, would be a huge step toward your own divinity;' thought Jesus with a bit of a wry smile. He now knew life after life, and living with your own soul, would be an important part of his teaching. Jesus excused himself, and went for a walk by himself that evening. There was so much to think about, he was trying to organize his thoughts. It seemed to him it was time to go home and begin his life's work. He knew now what it was he must do.

Forgetful of where he was going and so deep in thought he wandered back to that area where he had healed the little girl. Vishnu had often told him it was unwise to go out alone, especially in those parts of Ujjain where all the very poor lived. Looking about him, Jesus noted that there seemed to be a sudden end to the more prosperous housing and the beginning of shacks. Here on the edge of this village of the poor, he saw a boy sitting on the ground with a crude wooden bowl held out in front of him begging. It seemed obvious someone must have carried him to this place. Looking at the boy he realized there was little doubt he is placed here. Those thin twisted legs, would not have permitted him to walk here on his own. This child was being used by others to bring in money.

Jesus looked at him, his heart filling with compassion. He did not carry money or even food, to offer this child. From deep inside of him he heard the voice of God; Calling on him to help the boy to stand on his own. "Here is one who will one day, work for the very poor." Jesus hearing God's voice, was filled with compassion and love for this child. He reached down lifted him to his feet. The child reacted with terror, fearing he would be slapped as so often happened. When the boy saw the look of love and compassion on the face of this stranger his fear changed to wonder and surprise. Jesus held the boy upright, and speaking to God said; "Heal him, Oh Lord God, give him full use of his legs. Make them strong and complete, in the name of all that is good." The boy suddenly became aware of a new strength flowing into his legs. He could feel his feet for the first time, and then that strength flowed upward to his thighs. As Jesus took his hands away, the boy stood on his own for the first time in his life. A look of utter amazement appeared on his face. First, he slowly moved his feet, then to his amazement walked. First a few tentative steps, and then in total joy and wonderment he began to walk around in circles. A few on the street saw this miracle. They gathered around him, tentatively touching him, patting and uttering words of praise for this miracle man.

Vishnu had followed quietly behind. Always protective of his student, he moved to steer Jesus away from what was now a fast forming crowd. Before he left, Jesus placed his hand on the head of the boy while Vishnu spoke to him in his own language. Then the two quickly left. Walking away, Jesus touched Vishnu's arm and said; "May I ask what you said to that boy Master Vishnu?"

"Yes" Vishnu replied, I told him to thank God for his miracle and be prepared to help his people. He will become one of his countries great leaders." Jesus looking at the teacher and said, "How could you know that? Looking at Jesus with a little smile on his face, he replied; "That is what God said to me." Vishnu still smiling, looked at Jesus and continued; "God works his wonders in many mysterious ways. It is for us to believe and may expect to witness the glory of His power, when we are filled with His love."

As they walked along a pathway back home, Jesus took Vishnu once more by the arm pulling him to a stop, and said, "My good friend and teacher, I believe it is time for me to go back to where I came from." Vishnu said, "I agree."

# Chapter Fourteen

THE JOURNEY BACK home was long and tiring, Jesus knew it would be so, but it would give him time to collect his thoughts and prepare himself for the life ahead. Before Jesus left, and while each was saying a heartfelt goodbye, Vishnu handed Jesus a purse filled with money. "This is from your friends in little Israel, Ishmael, and myself. We wish you a safe journey, may God protect you and guide you along the way. I believe you are meant to become a great influence on this earth, both while you live and for a long time after."

As much as Jesus longed to once more be united with his family, saying goodbye to this wonderful old man was sad. Now approaching thirty years of age, Jesus was no longer the boy who ran away from home, he was a man in every sense of the word. He most certainly had matured in the past fourteen years, yet he still had that impetuous zeal of youth. His desire to fight greed and cruelty wherever he found it never wavered. His heart was with the unfortunate and always would be. Why can life on earth not be a joy for every person, he would say? Those born into poverty only to die in poverty would always be closest to his heart. He would constantly work for them wherever he found them. Alas, he suspected that wherever you find humanity there would be both rich and poor. With these thoughts, he could see why God's word needed to be taken far beyond the borders of Israel. Thinking of how the Buddha chose to spread his words, Jesus would need many helpers also.

As he walked along the hot and dusty road, he recounted his time with the Buddhist monks and their words. Both they and the Jains believed in a life without violence. Love and compassion were foremost in their lives. Most religions had similarities, yet unfortunately so many saw the differences before they opened their minds to the beliefs each shared.

As he travelled, he met others travelling the same path. Jesus found this most enjoyable. They would walk together, often camp together, and share what food and water they carried. So often when they camped for the night they would compare their experiences. Telling each about their lives and customs. Jesus had so much he could talk about, and noticed how his stories were received with such interest. There was no doubt he was a good speaker and getting better as time passed. Some of those travelling in the opposite direction, would bring stories from Israel and Judea. Jesus loved to hear such messages.

The journey was arduous, long and exhausting. His thoughts were constantly about his family and their welfare. It seemed that the agony he had supressed because of their separation was with him every step of the way. This took much out of him. He ached to be home, knowing there was much to be done. How would the family greet him when he arrived back in Nazareth? Had he have changed so much he might seem a stranger? His age had more than doubled since his last day in Jerusalem. No, he knew in his heart they would still love him and accept him. So, he trudged on.

At long last he entered Nazareth. His eyes sought familiar buildings and most importantly, familiar people. His heart beat faster as he drew closer to home and his excitement grew. Jesus recognized himself as an impatient man in most situations, but that impatience was growing by the minute now he was back in Nazareth. He walked faster. Scanning each face, looking for a loved one. One person called to him, "good day Thomas, you must be working harder than ever, you're losing weight." Jesus giggled at that remark. Then he rounded a corner and saw his mother's house. His heart seemed to leap into his throat. He was short of breath, and then he saw her standing by the door looking up the road, sheltering her eyes from the sun. He called out "mother." Mary could not believe her eyes, even though when she awoke that morning she felt this is the day.

She looked older, but then she was, fifteen years older. Her hair was grey, and yes there was a stoop in her posture, but this was Mary his mother. Now he really choked up. His heart could not beat any faster, but his legs ran faster. Tears filled his eyes. As she saw him she began to run toward him calling "Jesus, Oh, Jesus, I knew you were coming today, knew it, I just knew it." Then she was standing close with her arms around him, touching him, kissing him. "Oh, how I have missed you, but I knew you were in God's good hands and always safe". The words flowed out one after the other. Sometimes not totally coherent, but Jesus treasured every word she said. He found it hard to talk. Never the less this moment was everything he had hoped for. Here was his dear mother in his arms, and words were not necessary. He was home. Thank you, God.

Then the family were one again. Gathered together, enjoying the intimacy of this occasion. Special foods were prepared and served. When Jesus saw Ruth for the first time he looked at her face and remembered the little girl in Ujjeni. He stopped for a moment. In his mind, he reached out to God, and an unspoken prayer asked for a healing for his sister.

(Dear God, my father, if it be your will let her face be as she always hoped it would be.)

He touched her face with both hands, covering it completely. He could feel the change taking place beneath his fingers, as he kissed her forehead. As he removed his hands, all in the room expelled their breath as one. Everyone could hear the little gasp from Ruth as she heard their sounds. She could not know what was happening, but sensed something important had happened. When Jesus removed his hands from her face, even Jesus was amazed. For his sister, Ruth was transformed, she was indeed beautiful. The others gasped in utter astonishment, while Ruth not being able to see what had happened, knew something miraculous had occurred. She ran from the room to see for herself. Then sinking to her knees, sobbed.

The day ended with the family going to sleep thanking God. The miracle of Jesus returning, combined with the miracle of Ruth's face, would set the course for the path he was to follow.

They had spent the evening exchanging stories, of course it was Jesus who had the most to relate. James had been quiet, not knowing where his younger brother had been or what he had been doing, but finally accepting that his young man had changed. In his mind he asked changed into what? When he had witnessed the miracle with Ruth's face it was evident Jesus was no ordinary person, but then he admitted he never had been.

James had become a priest at the temple, working as a teacher, and highly respected. Also, he was married and now was a father. Secretly he wondered what the return of Jesus would do to his position. Knowing his brother was controversial to say the least. Would he antagonize the head priest and other leaders? Knowing his brother's passionate temperament, combined with his experiences while away, anything might happen.

Everything taken in to consideration, Thomas was overjoyed to have his brother back. He longed to get him away by himself, to hear more about his life since they parted. Of course, like everyone else in the family, wondered what his plans were, or did he have any? Jude had also married and lived here on the property. Ethyl and Jacob had died while Jesus was away, but their rooms were filled with a fast-growing family.

Last evening while the family recounted their own stories, Mary sat quietly, listening to the excited conversation, also thanking God repeatedly. Her wandering boy was back. As she looked at her twin boys she saw how identical they still were in appearance, yet so far apart in temperament. Thomas quiet, loving, understanding, and humble, he must be dearly loved by God. Jesus on the other hand was fiery, positive, and dedicated. He was truly God's man on earth. Where would his goals take him? What were his goals? What danger might lay before him? Her mother's love for her child, caused an involuntary shudder to pass through her. Quickly, she buried her fears, and just looked at him, loving him. This was a time for rejoicing, not fearing the future.

Jesus found Thomas's occupation as a boat builder interesting, he wished to learn more about this occupation. He suggested Thomas spend a day with him to discuss some ideas he had. The boat building and its location seemed to foster an abstract idea. Or at least the people involved in and around the sea. If you asked him what it was he was thinking, he would truthfully tell you he had no idea, and that was true, he didn't. As these thoughts floated about in his head he was asking himself if this train of thoughts might be more of Gods guidance. Oh yes, it must be, he would ask God before he slept tonight.

The next day as Thomas and Jesus walked together, Jesus told his brother how a soul and a person must be one. First explaining about the soul that joined each person at birth and the closeness of each soul to God. "Our souls are who we really are. I must teach this to all who will listen. This is what he believed God wanted him to do. The brothers sat side by side while Jesus explained to Thomas much of what he had learned, and he had grown spiritually. He told him of Ishmael and Vishnu, and how they contributed so much to his learning experiences. "Travel to the sea with me Thomas, introduce me to your friends and we will start there. Thomas, I want you to come and work with me, help me to do God's work. Together we will change the world." Thomas' head was swimming with the excitement and the passion of his brother. Then Jesus went on to discuss the importance of recruiting others to help spread the message. "We cannot do it alone," he said; "It will be necessary to recruit disciples and teach them. You will be my first, Thomas my dear brother. God wishes us to tell every one of his love and forgiveness. He wants us to speak out against greed, and above all help people to understand our souls and our body must live as one so we move on to everlasting life in that soul. Our souls all come from the same place and are all equal in Gods eyes. Our task will be to take this, God's message, to all the people."

With Thomas' agreement, Jesus and his brother found themselves by the sea. Here Jesus saw first-hand what work his brother did, and had a chance to meet others who worked there. Jesus never knew why, but the type of people whom he found here represented the type of individual he would draw on for his followers. Thomas introduced Jesus to many of his friends. They were interested in his travels and what he learned about other countries and their beliefs. Jesus told them of their customs and way of living. It was not long before a small group gathered together, and Jesus found himself talking where he had been and about how greed was as prevalent there as it was here. How armies would sweep in and take over a country, bringing new ways of finding God. Despite what others called their God or what they saw as God, there was only one God for all people, no matter what race or country. He discussed with them their own souls and how it was important to live the way God would have us live, and then he told them about life after life. He told them how the Buddha strove to find a way to live to avoid coming back over and over. Gently introducing them to life after death and the wonder of knowing that when their bodies died they lived on.

Day after day he talked and taught, and as he did so the crowds grew larger. It was not long before his message, passion, his voice, and his fame as a rabbi teacher grew.

Weeks became months, and the word of this man who spoke a new truth spread throughout the land. He talked of how each person's soul was a part of God. When you ignore your soul, you ignore God.

Occasionally he would heal someone who was suffering. As he met those with serious afflictions his heart went out to them. He would go on to explain why it was necessary to come back to earth to be born again, and help others find Gods way. He often referred to the Buddha who, also despised greed. As God forgives you, so you should forgive each other. Some would ask if he worshipped the Buddha and Jesus answered no, the Buddha is not a God, but a prophet who wanted to ease the suffering of people while on earth.

One time as he was talking to a crowd of people about the word of God, two women named Martha and Mary Magdalene left the group and came forward to greet him. He had noticed them in the crowds before. It had been his intention after finishing one day, to single them out and speak to them. They had heard his messages several times, and now Mary told Jesus his words had great meaning to her. She wished to become a disciple. Jesus eagerly accepted her. After Thomas, she was the second to become one of his followers. The three, Jesus, Thomas and Mary spent a lot of time together. Sometimes when the three were alone, perhaps sitting and eating he would talk of his years in India and the caste system he saw there. He then compared it to the same thing he saw in Jerusalem. Caiaphas the high priest, saw differences in their own people. He singled out the Pharisees and the Sadducee. This prompted Jesus to say when you divide a kingdom you divide the love of one for the other. God means for all people to respect and care for each other, even though they live in other countries. Those who would invade other counties for the sake of riches and land, have turned their back on God.

He added new disciples when Mathew, James, and John stepped out from the crowd and asked to become part of the Rabbi's followers. You have made us believers, they told him. It was not long after that Peter and Andrew came to Jesus, and said we have heard what you say and would be part of those who spread the word. Thomas had known Peter and Andrew for some time. They were fishermen and met Thomas the builder of boats, and in this found a commonality. It turned out they had stood in the first group, when Jesus had spoken, and now after hearing Jesus speak again, they knew what they must do.

Soon the group had become twelve plus Jesus. They were invited to a large home for dinner along with many others. The gathering was large, the food was excellent, and the wine was the very best. These were people who used currency to buy all their needs including friendship and favours. Jesus was aware of this and while his views on currency had softened somewhat during his years away, he still clung to his old beliefs. Where money is found, you will find greed.

The disparity between those with much and those with little or none, only strengthened. His trip home could not have worked as well as it did without money and for this he was grateful. He never could understand why a person could hoard money just for the sake of owning it. Money tends to promote greed he would tell them. Those with more than they need should be helping those without. The world would not or could not function without a medium of exchange today, but remember Jesus was raised in a village that worked much like a commune.

While Jesus and his disciples were at the dinner, he was asked to speak to the gathering. He talked to them about the very poor he had seen in a far-off country. He recalled his experience's in lucid detail, painting a picture in words of those incidents that he now remembered so well.

They heard how it was necessary to beg for mere scraps. Children forced to stand outside with their bowls, exhibiting their deformities and often showing evidence of beatings. He told again of the Buddha who had been a prince, and gave it all up when he saw the sick, the poor and the destitute. In the telling he went on to discuss the task of the soul and how its task was to remind the human mind to care for the poor and feeble. Those gathered learned how the soul when after leaving the body, would later be judged on its success or lack of it in guiding the human along God's way. The conversation eventually led to the soul of each person in the room and its relationship with God. Listen to what I tell you it is not too late to save yourself. His voice deepened, and his eyes flashed, as he pointed at the group. Love your neighbour and love your enemy, he shouted now. Learn to forgive, be charitable. To many forgiveness was a new thought.

To answer their questions, it was necessary for Jesus repeat over again how a soul comes from heaven to live in a body at the time of birth. The soul wishes to guide the human brain to live a fruitful and helpful life. Sometimes, the soul becomes so human it becomes more a part of humanity than part of God. Now the soul becomes discontented, wants more, possesses more, eventually it encourages the human to take from others to accumulate money just for the sake of owning it, thus loses its contact with God. When that body becomes dust, the soul must return to where it came from, and there in the presence of perfection, it must be judged.

In the group was an elder from the synagogue in Jerusalem, who went back to the high priest Caiaphas with the news of this rabbi. He told him of this man who was preaching contrary to the holy law. He related the message Jesus preached to Caiaphas and the elders who had gathered together to hear this report. They listened in shock and railed out in anger at this blasphemy. Who is this so-called rabbi who speaks such words? He must be brought to justice. They had the elder repeat the message over and over.

Thus, began a resentment that would put fear in the hearts of the high priest and his elders. The foundation for the charges which would eventually be laid against Jesus, were prepared in that room. As if this elder had not said enough he added, "This man said we are all equal in the eyes of God, even Gentiles and Romans.

"The die was cast.

# Chapter Fifteen

"THERE IS NO need to feel alone and frightened when God and his mercy are part of our lives," Jesus was standing on the side of a hill, speaking to a group of followers. He found a spot under a tree, and talked to one of the largest groups he had ever attracted. "Live with God in your life, and you will never be alone. Remember greed is the way of evil, and evil leads to self-destruction. If you look at beggars and turn your back, you are living without God. When your day has come to leave this world, you must go back to where you came from, and be judged. Seek the Kingdom of God now, while you are here in this life, and live forever in that Holy Place with God."

One person in the crowd called out, "Master where is this Kingdom you speak of, how would I find it"? Jesus stopped his words and looked out to see the originator of that question, "Look around you. Open your mind, the Kingdom of God is here within you. You need only open your mind and be guided by your soul."

Whenever and wherever he spoke, those who heard him became believers. This success, unfortunately is what caused the High Priest and rabbis to act. It would seal his doom.

As the crowds became followers in ever increasing numbers, information relating to the activities and words of Jesus were constantly reported to the high priest Caiaphas. That powerful person would fly into a rage. A rage that only increased his determination to rid himself and the world of this man. He would never admit it to those around him, but along with his anger there was also a deepening fear he was being threatened. "What utter nonsense," he would tell himself that cannot happen, but the doubt would not leave him.

As Caiaphas pondered this large question, he admitted to himself it would weaken his position if this one man were seen to frighten him or even worry him. While his mind chewed on the issue, a new thought came to him. Why not seek help, someone with power who could take the responsibility of the action he had in mind? One who might benefit by the removal of this man Jesus. There was no better person than Pilate the commanding officer of the Roman army. Since Herod had died and his weak son had taken his place, Pilates power had grown. As the High Priests thoughts warmed to his plan he knew there were other reasons Pilate might be very agreeable. There were rumours coming back from Rome about a feeling of antisemitism that had been growing. Leaders in the senate were calling on the Emperor to be harder on the Jews. People who had travelled to Jerusalem had come back with a feeling of resentment. After seeing the temple in all its glory, they became angry because only Jews were allowed in. There were calls to rip it down. These Jews are getting too big for their own good. However, the emperor hesitated to stir up another revolt. He sent orders to Pilate to maintain the peace. Avoid any kind of trouble or any trouble maker that might upset the balance.

Ever the politician, Pilate had disguised a large troop of soldiers as Jews, and had hidden weapons in their robes, then infiltrated those who had gathered in the temple to protest the Roman army. The soldiers created a riot and killed many of the protestors. All of this resulted in unrest when it was discovered by survivors what Roman soldiers had done. The people were angry, rebellious and calling for justice. Obviously, this had been a mistake on the part of Pilate, a man who never made mistakes. He remembered, it was not long ago that a man named Simon had rebelled and needed to be subdued. Pilate did not want another rebellion.

The high priest asked himself, could this man Jesus be presented as a threat to the Roman leader? Perhaps if it was put to him in the right way this would be an opportunity. Pilate could ingratiate himself with Tiberius once again, by ridding another Jewish troublemaker from his jurisdiction. It would be necessary to present it to him in such a way he would see that Jesus was a threat to Rome itself. The cunning mind of the high priest wrestled with this thought, knowing it would need to be handled skillfully.

There was another matter that was of concern to Caiaphas. A situation of severe importance. The Sanhedrin. This was a council of over seventy members dominated by the Pharisees. Their mandate was to guide both Pilate and Caiaphas on matters of civic and cultic importance. They annoyed the high priest by interfering with matters in the temple. Primarily the sale of sacrificial animals to the public for sacrifice. Their single-mindedness to the old laws was almost fanatical. They left no room for Caiaphas to manipulate the Temple's management to his benefit. Yes, he needed the power and backing of the Roman army. There was little doubt in Caiaphas mind that Pilate would be aware of Jesus and his influence in the community. That Roman soldier missed nothing.

Dealing with the Sanhedrin was a delicate matter. After all they were the watchdogs of the Jewish law, but too many were considered extremists. Money was not permitted in the Temple itself, that, was Pharisees teaching, but to buy a sacrifice in the great court, and that is considered part of the Temple, turned the building into a market place. Caiaphas disagreed. How could the Temple be what it is, without the profits generated by the merchant's? Any fool knows that. To make matters worse, this was one of the points the man Jesus preached against. Another reason to get rid of him. Jesus had heard of Pilate's deception and massacre of innocent Jews. In his forthright manner, he called upon both Caiaphas and Pilate to be held accountable for this tragedy. To make matters worse, people were listening to this out of control Rabbi. When you added up all these points, it was clear, Jesus must go.

Trouble was mounting for Jesus, and in the disciples point of view, he did nothing to soften the anger he was building against himself.

As his brother, and, as a disciple I had always said the stubborn streak of Jesus would get him into trouble. When I pointed this out to him, Jesus put his hands on my shoulders and looking me in the eye said; maybe that is why I am here, doing what I must do! Thomas.

So, it must happen, this the most powerful Jew in Israel, would take steps to rid himself of two thorns in his side. Caiaphas would move the Sanhedrin away to nearby Mount Olive and out of the Temple with the support of this powerful Roman. The trouble maker Jesus would be arrested by Pilate. Even if that troublesome Roman did not know it yet, he soon would. Caiaphas chuckled at his own cleverness.

A meeting with Pilate was arranged. When the Roman leader asked, what the agenda for this meeting consisted of, he was advised, both the Sanhedrin and the trouble maker Jesus were to be discussed.

Pilate and Caiaphas were about to become allies. Neither liked the other, but necessity brings many alike people together. Pilate ordered the meeting at his headquarters, this irked Caiaphas not a little. He would have loved Pilate to have come to him, even though it would be bringing a Roman into the temple.

Jesus had chosen to move his teaching to Jerusalem and the Temple itself. He knew this to be a dangerous step, but the word of God must be told everywhere. Jerusalem was the largest city, so here were to be found, the most converts.

I called upon my brother to heed the growing danger, but he told me if he was to accomplish God's work there was no turning back. I knew he talked to God regularly, but it seemed to myself and the other disciples, caution was advisable. I talked to Mary Magdalene about my concerns because she seemed to understand Jesus better than myself and the others. Mary was as concerned as all the rest of us, but she said; Jesus knows best, he talks to God daily.

Therefore, we all went to the Temple once more. I suggested to Mary Magdalene, there could be danger and perhaps she should stay away. She said her place was with Jesus.

On the way up the hill, Jesus accosted the merchants, and told them to take their business elsewhere. This is the house of the Lord not a place of business. I suppose Jesus knew his outburst was useless, but he felt it was good for the visitors who stood nearby. The merchants sat quietly while he spoke. They did not bother to respond they did not need to. Why pay attention to this so-called Rabbi? The high priest received a portion of their profits, so when they had a problem they complained to the authorities.

Jesus condemned the use and needless slaughter of animals, which also produced an income to both the high priest and his associates. Once more this radical preacher was a subject of derision by those whose life depended upon commerce. Regardless of the tension that was mounting, Jesus stood on the steps and spoke to all who would stop and listen. There were many. People eagerly surrounded him to listen to his words.

The high priest was fully aware that the man from Nazareth was in the temple. Rather than confront him, he chose to stay back and listen. He had never heard Jesus speak. Despite having been told the man was a powerful speaker, the high priest was amazed at how he held the crowd's attention. This was a chance for him to see and hear what this man Jesus was telling those in his audience. Standing away from the group but close enough to hear, he heard him say; "All men are equal in the eyes of God. God dwells in the heart of all people no matter what their beliefs. When we are born, our soul enters the body and lives with us for our entire lives. That soul is us, you and me. We are that soul. The body is merely a temporary dwelling place. When you choose the path of greed and are not charitable you ignore the will of God. Money is the tool of the greedy, and brings evil into the hearts of those who would see it as their God. You must share with those who have nothing. Love thy neighbour as thyself no matter what his or her race or religion. Forgive your enemies we are all equal in His eyes." These words fell upon the ears of the priests and elders like a blow. Caiaphas standing behind a pillar heard it all. He joined the crowd now and moved to accost Jesus, asking him by what authority does he preach in this holy place? Jesus quietly replied.

"The Lord himself asked me.

"Do you say the Lord God speaks to you."

"Yes." Jesus said. He would speak to you also, if you speak sincerely with love in your heart"

If Caiaphas needed anything more to convince him of the need to rid the world of this man, these words decided his fate. There was no turning back.

# Chapter Sixteen

THE FATEFUL MEETING between the powers, took place on a warm day. The smell of the season was in the air, and everything considered, this meeting should be productive. At least that was the way Caiaphas expected it would turn out. As he entered the luxurious surroundings, he tried not to let it be too obvious as he looked about. The offices of Pilate were very impressive. The high priest sniffed as he saw that the Captain's man had put out food and drink. He was still smarting and neither his mood nor his ego were likely to improve. All of this because; upon entering, two smartly dressed soldiers crossed their spears and refused him entrance until their leader bade them allow the chief priest to enter. Once in the great man's presence, civilities over, and food declined, Pilate listened to all Caiaphas had to say. Then looking at this temple official, he shrugged his shoulders and said, "Do as you wish."

Caiaphas was not through, and not ready to be shrugged off lightly. He asked if Pilate knew of the man Jesus he had been talking about. 'Yes' the captain responded. 'I am aware of this man, I have been hearing talk, and sent some of my people to listen. Actually, some of the things the rabbi Jesus said were quite interesting." Those words fell on the high priest's ears like personal blows. His hatred for the man grew to a hot point. Nothing more could be gained by remaining longer, he looked at the food shrugged his shoulders and left.

We disciple's, knew that tension with the authorities was mounting, and should not be discounted. We could feel it in the air. It was all around us. Even those who normally followed us seemed uneasy. We all begged Jesus to go away for a while and save himself. Jesus looked at us as we gathered round him and said; "To run away would undo all we have accomplished. We must trust that my remaining here is what the Lord God would wish.

Information eventually reach us as we gathered at the home of a friend that an order for the arrest of Jesus had been given to the command post. News attributed to Caiaphas himself; "The man Jesus preached against Jewish law and that is treason". It had been reported the so called rabbi Jesus also said; We are all born equal, even the Romans, that statement alone makes him a criminal."

When Jesus heard the words attributed to the high priest, he responded by saying, "I was born a Jew and I remain a Jew. I live by Jewish law, but I do not recognize all that this local counsel claims to be law. They misinterpret the law to make it work for their own benefit. The God we worship is the same God all worship, no matter what they call him. There is but one God. If some find what I say to be wrong, let them tell it to the Lord God themselves. If God comes to me and tells me I am wrong, I will stop my preaching and teaching and just go away."

On the first day of the feast of unleavened bread, we asked Jesus where he wished to eat the Passover. Jesus said we have all been invited to celebrate the Passover with a friend at his home. With those words, we set off for this friend's house. Later, Jesus gathered us all together and said; "We must take some time to plan ahead. Danger is at hand and changes are about to happen. We have discussed what each will do if I am no longer here. You will all continue to preach Gods word as I have done. It is likely I will be arrested and taken away. I do not know how long they will keep me. I want you to remember, the word of God must be taken to faraway places as well as continuing the teaching here. God is with you as He is with me. We have discussed where each of you will go, but whatever place you go to, please remember my heart is with you always."

It was that night Pilates soldiers came and took Jesus away to stand before Caiaphas his priests and elders. They sat as a jury, to charge him and try him. Witnesses were called to testify for or against him. They were asked if Jesus had said all were equal in the eyes of God, and they answered yes. They testified he said unless you love and share with each other no matter who they may be, you deprive the Lord. If you fail in this you must be born again, to come back to earth to live your life all over. Through all this Jesus remained silent.

Caiaphas asked him, "Do you deny these words."

Jesus said, "No, I do not deny them, they are true."

"Do you also say we are all one with God, and God loves all of us?"

Jesus answered; "I do not deny it."

Caiaphas arose from his chair, placing his hands on the table in front of him. He then looked at the priests, rabbis, and elders, the jury who would decide the fate of Jesus. A look of satisfaction shone on his face, clearly showing the triumph, he felt at this moment. Then raising his hand to gain attention, he said, "You have heard it, how do you say? The jurors answered. "Guilty." Let him suffer death.

There was no discussion amongst them. It appeared the guilty verdict had been decided before the trial began. The next morning the council met to approve the death warrant.

Death by hanging on the cross.

Jesus had been bound and led away the day before. The jailors had not fed him or even gave him water on orders of the high priest. With food in his stomach, he might have vomited while on the cross, which could arouse sympathy among those in attendance.

One more step remained. By Roman rule, Pilate himself must refuse or approve the punishment. Caiaphas worried crucifixion might not be approved. This part was important, if an end to the threat arising from this man's teaching is to cease. The guards went to Jesus and he was marched before the Roman leader.

Caiaphas looked at Jesus and said, "Are you the one who calls himself the Son of God?

Do you say, all are equal in the eyes of God?

Jesus looked him in the eye and said, "Yeah it is so. There is but one God, and he resides in the heart of all of us. We are all children of Him, and all are equal in His eyes. Thus, I say to you, if God sees us as equals, must we not do the same?

Pilate arose from his chair, where he had watched the trial and said; "There is nothing I can do, take him away and do as you will."

# CHAPTER SEVENTEEN

IT WAS A procession such as Jerusalem had never seen before, soldiers, rabbis, and elders all walking together, with Jesus in the middle. His hands were tied in front of him, his head held high. They walked him through the streets crowds lining the entire way. Pushing and shoving to get to the front. They jeered and hurled insults at him. More soldiers stood amidst the crowds to keep control. Many of those now calling out for his death were the ones who spent hours listening to his teaching. It would seem they had forgotten his words as they now cried for his blood. Some wept with compassion and anguish at the same time praying for his deliverance. A tourist named Simon, had been pulled from the street by the soldiers and commanded to carry the cross. It was necessary for him to drag it on the ground because it was just too heavy to carry.

Jesus saw and heard the cries from some of the people. He recognised many as those who once called him master. As the odd stone hit him he thought back to the street entertainer, who had walked on live coals. He remembered the man's words, when he told Jesus how to deal with pain; "You go into your inner self, that part of you that is beyond the body, there to find your soul. It is there no one can hurt you. "When pain is the worst," he had said, "your heart will slow and almost stop." As Jesus recalled those words he thought; that will stop the physical pain, but in the heart, there is greater pain. A pain caused by those out of control people screaming for his death. Why had so many of those who had called him rabbi and listened to his words, now turn their back on him?

The family stood along the way the procession must pass, tears were welling up in our eyes, but when Jesus came abreast of us, we saw there were also tears in his eyes. We knew the tears he wept were out of anguish for our suffering. Mother, Mary Magdalene, James, Jude, Ruth, and myself were in a state of shock none of us believed this could happen. "Perhaps at the last moment he sent out of the country, but not hurt." We never believed what we now were seeing would never end in his death. We prayed for a miracle praying for God to save him. All the disciples along with friends were among the throng. They too could not believe that Caiaphas the high priest, wanted him dead. How could he a Jew, one who had decried the blood the Romans had shed, would himself turn to the same bloody way?

All of us were unable to believe there would not be a last-minute intervention by God. The lips of Jesus were moving as he looked at us. I knew he was praying for us. Finally, in a place called Golgotha, meaning place of the skull they stopped. Here Simon the cross bearer could put down his burden. He then fled through the crowd, never to return to this city again. "They are barbarians he told himself."

My mother and Mary Magdalene told myself, Ruth, and Jude to go home immediately. Leave this area now. The said because of my identical appearance to Jesus, it is unsafe to remain here. This was no place for Ruth and Jude either. With the mood of the crowd, anything could happen. Jude and Ruth were beside themselves with the horror of what was happening. "Why do people do this to others, why does God allow this to happen?" Jude sobbed as I led them away.

I explained to them what Jesus had told me. "We have total freedom to use our time on earth as we wish. That is what God tells all souls before they leave heaven. We know God wants all humans to treat others as they wish to be treated. Live with love, compassion, and generosity to those without. When we do this, all is well. Do not kill, but embrace the unfortunate and forgive those who do evil. We knew this before we came to earth to live in a human body. When we hate, hurt, and slander others, we will suffer for it when we return home, to be judged." I told them once more.

When the procession reached the hill, Jesus was fastened to the cross. It was lifted upright and dropped into a hole in the ground. It was the custom to break the legs of the criminals. They do this, so they cannot hold themselves upright, and thus the weight of the body would collapse the lungs and cause the victim to die of suffocation. For some reason this was not done with Jesus. This allowed him to hold himself up using the footplate under his feet. Later we reasoned the elders hoped death would be prolonged and more painful. Who knows? The hatred that had welled up since his arrest was beyond understanding.

The priests certainly looked pleased with the way it was all proceeding. It had gone as planned. Caiaphas had accomplished what he set out to do. This threat to his power had been done away with.

Many in the crowd had brought lunches, and chose this moment to bring the food out. They sat quietly on the ground and ate while they waited for Jesus to die.

With the cross now in place and Jesus high above the people, he prayed to God asking for his forgiveness and blessing for those who were doing this. As well he said; "My father, forgive me my arrogance and know of my love." He heard the voice of God reply, "You have fulfilled my every wish and I am greatly pleased. I promise you will never need to come back to this earth again in human form." With that the head of Jesus slumped over, the crowd thinking he was dead began to leave. There was a great stillness among them as they slowly left the hill.

Later when everyone was gone except a few soldiers, I came back and knelt at the foot of the cross weeping, I called out to him.

"Jesus, I love you so, and I do not want you to be gone."

To my utter astonishment, I heard Jesus speaking very quietly to me.

"Thomas, shed no tears, this is not over. I promise from all of this will come the pathway to save the world."

I cannot explain how I felt at that moment, but before I could think further James appeared with some friends and said; We have a place for his body, help us lift the cross and take him from it. With that we laid the cross flat and removed the nails that penetrated his body. We very gently moved him to a small cave that had been set aside as a tomb. Here we placed his body, and all together moved a large stone over the entrance. The soldiers had followed us, and their commander ordered two soldiers to stand guard and not allow anyone to enter. Then he told us; "This is the least we can do, I feel a great wrong has been done today.

When all had gone and the area still, there inside that cold and damp cave, the heart of Jesus began to slowly beat faster, life flowed through his body. God sent healing to stop the bleeding and pain. After this Jesus heard the voice of God once more saying, "My son your work here is done, go far away and experience life as a normal human and have many years of happiness. Your life will never be forgotten and will be an example of how one should live on this earth. Your memory and your messages will be a comfort for many in this world."

Later during the night, the light of the moon became so brilliant it lit up the entrance to the cave and all around it. The brightness was so vivid it frightened the two guards who trembled in fear and ran away crying; "What have we done?" The heavy stone slowly began to roll away completely on its own.

Then Jesus walked out. As he left the cave, Mary his mother, and Mary Magdalene, arrived. They had been drawn back to the site by a strong feeling they both had. A sense they were unable to explain even to each other. They never could have expected what their eyes now beheld. For before them was the figure of Jesus walking out of the cave entrance. Shock, fear and confusion overtook them. Stunned beyond belief, they held each other, hardly able to breath or comprehend what they saw. They stayed this way until slowly full realization filled them with joy.

Jesus was alive.

Mary Magdalene was the first to rush toward him and wrap a robe around his body. Quickly their joy turned to concern. They did not understand what had happened, but knew Jesus was not safe yet, further action must take place. Swiftly they hurried him away, lest others should appear. "This is truly the work of God" Mary said to Jesus. "But now we must flee immediately. If they find you they will chop, you to pieces." The way was painfully slow. Jesus was so very weak, his legs trembling as he took each step. She led the little procession to a friend of hers, where they told those inside it is Thomas, the brother of Jesus who is ill. "We must tend to him," Mary said. There they stayed until James found a donkey and cart and took Jesus back home to Nazareth, where he remained until he was well enough to travel.

Mary Magdalene arranged for Jesus to meet with the disciples. They could not believe this was real until Jesus showed his scars. "As you see I live. I have returned from the grave. The power of the Lord God now calls you to take over my work. Carry on as we planned. Go to all the countries we have discussed. Tell the truth as you know it to all people. The Holy Spirit is with you. Go, teach and heal, for this, you can do. I will go away, and you will never see me again. You must understand for me to stay here will undo all we have accomplished. The high priest and his elders must never know I live. The job is now yours. Never doubt you can do all I have done, and more, for you walk with the power of God within you.

Now it was time for us to leave. I accompanied Jesus and Mary Magdalene to the sea, where I arranged for us to go by boat to the far shore of a place now called Marseilles. There they would be safe and able to do as God had said. Go and live a normal life.

During this voyage, Jesus and I wrote a book of his sayings, you may know as the Gospel of Thomas. I took it with me when I left them and traveled east, eventually stopping in India. I never saw my brother and Mary again. I do know they found sanctuary in the land you now call France. Here they lived in peace where they had three children and many grandchildren. Jesus lived to be more than eighty years of age. God promised Jesus an opportunity to live as a normal human. A husband and father. To love and be loved, in the bosom of his family, until the time came to leave his human body and go home to God the Father. Mary, his wife, and mother of his children, followed less than three years later.

# Epilogue

THERE YOU HAVE it. As I said, I believe every word of what I have written here. I believe I was guided to write what I did. There is so much here that contradicts the established Christian doctrine. Why would God choose me? Why did he choose Abraham to have children when he was over one hundred years old?

I leave it to the reader to decide.

www.ingramcontent.com/pod-product-compliance
Lightning Source LLC
Chambersburg PA
CBHW052151110526
44591CB00012B/1941